DRAWING AND MODELMAKING

DRAWING AND MODELMAKING

BY ALEXANDER RATENSKY

WHITNEY LIBRARY OF DESIGN
an imprint of Watson-Guptill Publications/New York

First published 1983 in New York by Whitney Library of Design,
an imprint of Watson-Guptill Publications,
a division of Billboard Publications, Inc.,
1515 Broadway, New York, N.Y. 10036

Library of Congress Cataloging in Publication Data
Ratensky, Alexander
  Drawing and modelmaking.
  Bibliography: p.
  Includes index.
  1. Architectural drawing—Technique. 2. Architec-
tural models. I. Title.
NA2708.R38 1983   720′.28′4   83-1164
ISBN 0-8230-7369-6

Distributed in the United Kingdom by Phaidon Press Ltd., Littlegate
House, St. Ebbe's St., Oxford

Manufactured in U.S.A.

First Printing, 1983

2 3 4 5 6 7 8 9/89 88 87 86

ACKNOWLEDGMENTS

I thank my many students from the past nine years for major contributions to this book. Teaching requires that we make clear what we know, but students help us see what to teach.

Architecture is an apprenticeship profession, and the habit of sharing knowledge is ingrained in most architects. Colleagues who have helped me over the years are too numerous to list, but the following need particular thanks: Harvey Kagan, Richard Snibbe, Andrew Cutler, Hugh Spence, and David Elwell. Carmi Bee has not only taught me a great deal over the years of our friendship, but also read this book in manuscript and made several valuable suggestions. David Evan Glasser, a teaching colleague for several years, was my collaborator in developing the freshman course that underlies much of what is here.

I am grateful to my former student and teaching assistant Susan Gardner, who insisted that I do this book and introduced me to my publishers.

Stephen A. Kliment and Susan Davis have been excellent and supportive editors. Their many contributions make this a better book than it would otherwise have been.

Finally, I want to thank my wife and sons for tolerating the major disruption in our lives that the writing and illustrating of a book created.

CONTENTS

PREFACE

The purpose of design drawing is communication. This primary intention is often lost sight of. It is easy to overlook: good drawings are pleasing artifacts in themselves and in an uncertain world may have to serve as the end product of the design process. But recognizing their purpose—to communicate ideas and information—may well change your approach to learning to draw.

Beyond communication lie other purposes. Drawings can convince, and in fact design drawing is really propaganda. Certainly part of our work is to show that what we design solves some problem and that what we propose is better than the alternatives.

Drawings can record. We draw to preserve our two- and three-dimensional thinking. Such drawings are made to communicate with ourselves, for ideas and mental images flee or are overlaid with later ideas. They are evidence, when we come back to check days or weeks or months or years later, of what we were thinking at some moment in time. Drawings preserve the flow of ideas, the development of solutions. They map a process that is only partially verbal and cannot ever be securely recorded in any other way.

Drawings can inform, and such drawing fills much of our lives. How to build it? What materials to use? How big to make it? How do pieces relate? What will it look like? These are drawings that teach.

Finally, of course, drawings can please. There is a sensual pleasure in drawing. In the same way that language can please, can extend our reach beyond the physical realm of the body into the world of ideas, so too can drawing widen that world to include purely visual thinking. We can learn to draw for the pure pleasure of enlarging our intellectual scope.

This is a book by an architect who teaches and who has taught people how to prepare design drawings for many years. The book is aimed at today's typical design student—someone who has come to the field after a period of searching, who may already have tried and succeeded at another profession, but who has not been prepared from childhood on for visual communication. Such a student will find classmates who draw with great facility and intuitive knowledge. He or she may feel daunted by their skill. These people almost certainly learned to draw as children. Their skills and intuitions are honed by experience almost to the point of being reflexive. This should not cause anxiety. Such ability is neither essential to being a student nor essential to succeeding as a design professional.

I teach the very basics here—the things my students have taught me need to be taught. At least some of what follows I learned as an apprentice or junior drafter in offices. The apprenticeship route into the design professions is less available now than it was twenty years ago, with the result that drawing instruction in schools needs to start with the basics. Students want to be taught how to hold the pencil, how to point it, how to construct a plan or section, how to survive in school, and how to develop skills that will land them jobs.

What makes this book different from the many others on the same subject is its focus on process, on the step-by-step build-up of a drawing. This approach is one my students have taught me is needed. The illustrations in most books on drawing include both the final drawing and its construction lines. The evolutionary stages of the drawings are obscured by the many additional lines of later steps. Such drawings require deciphering by beginners and therefore are frequently frustrating. Here we will separate the construction of the various drawings architects and designers most often use into individually illustrated steps. The process of construction will be emphasized rather than the final product.

CHAPTER ONE

THE BASIC TOOLS AND MATERIALS

This book is primarily about drawings made with tools. Drafted drawings. Such drawings characterize design drawing, that is, work intended for construction (or fabrication). They are also required for presentations made in schools, where a rigorous thought process is demanded. Drafted drawings, in that they are measured, have a precision of intent. Sketching, in this context, can be thought of as a precursor to drawing with tools. Of course, sketching is much more than that—it is an intrinsic part of the process of design—but drafted drawings are the working-out of designs, the realization of the concepts previously sketched. Even freehand design presentation drawings are usually prepared as tracings of a drafted drawing.

It will be useful before we go any further to define what we mean by drawing, sketching, and drafting. Drawing is the act of representing an object with lines and sometimes tones that are manually created. This therefore includes both drafting and sketching. Sketching is drawing by hand and pencil, without using other tools and without wholly copying or tracing another drawing. Note that a sketch may be partly traced, but it must somewhere involve new thought. Even if it is partly traced it represents a developing idea, which grew out of what was drawn before. Drafting is the creation of drawings with the tools about to be described, that is, t-squares and triangles. Presentation drawings may be: sketches, if they help explain the development of your thinking; drafted drawings, if the design is sufficiently refined to be best explained by them; or freehand tracings over previously drafted drawings. (These are not, therefore, sketches.)

The tools of drafted drawings need to be described—there are many, with a legion of choice. If you don't already own the tools, you should plan carefully how to proceed. Get yourself a good general drafting-supplies catalog, and study it. Manufacturers' catalogs, while fascinating, don't give a view of the whole field nor of current prices. A general catalog will carry many manufacturers' products. Several companies that offer general catalogs are listed in the Selected Bibliography. Only a small portion of what is available is needed from day to day.

On the following pages is a short description of the various tools in a basic kit needed to make design drawings. The particular makes or brands mentioned are those I have found through experience to be the best for my use and modest budget. Obviously, each person has preferences. In the chapters that follow, I will describe my use to help you understand how I made my choices. [If you are a student, your teacher(s) may well have different recommendations.]

THE DRAWING SURFACE

The first piece of equipment you'll need is a drawing table or board. It should have a surface that is flat and smooth and at least one edge that is straight and square, though this is essential only if you're going to use a t-square. The question of what size to get is important, because you don't want to buy twice, though there is no right answer for everyone. I enjoy working on a surface that is 37″ × 48″, a standard size. The biggest drawing I can produce on this board is 36″ × 48″. Meanwhile, the board and table fit quite comfortably in a modern apartment. Larger boards are useful if you have to produce larger drawings, as offices routinely do. However, the length of your arms becomes a factor here. We are concerned in this book with school-type drawings, and 36″ × 48″ should be large enough. I conduct my personal practice with drawings of this size and smaller.

You'll need to cover the drawing surface in some way so that you don't gouge it with your pencil (and ruin the drawing you're working on at the same time). A good, inexpensive cover is Laminene, made by Keuffel and Esser (K & E). It is a heavy, plain or gridded paper with an acetate coating. Buy it larger than the drawing surface by at least 6″ in each dimension. Wet it thoroughly in your bathtub and place it face down on a large towel. Place the board face down on top of the paper, and carefully wrap the paper around the edges of the board. Staple it to the board's underside. Be careful doing this. It is easy to tear the wet paper, which will shrink tight and smooth as it dries. Remember not to cover the edge you will be using your t-square on.

A more expensive alternative, although much easier to apply, is a board cover made of vinyl especially for this purpose. It is held in place by double-stick tape, which should be used only at the four edges of the top surface. The vinyl doesn't wrap to the underside.

The drawing surface is usually positioned higher above the floor than a standard desk, and architects and designers therefore normally draw while sitting on tall stools. The extra elevation of the drawing surface allows the drafter to draw while standing or sitting. A too-low table makes one bend over the board to work, inevitably resulting in neck and back strain as the hours progress.

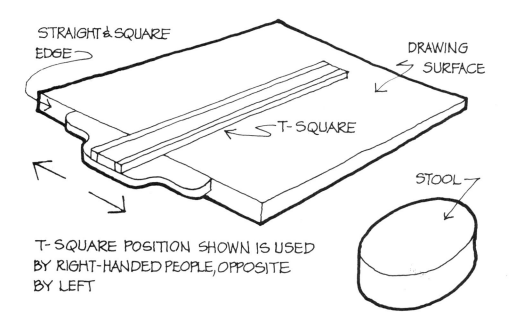

STRAIGHT & SQUARE EDGE

DRAWING SURFACE

T-SQUARE

STOOL

T-SQUARE POSITION SHOWN IS USED BY RIGHT-HANDED PEOPLE, OPPOSITE BY LEFT

LIGHTING

Once you've set up your drawing table or surface, you'll need to light it properly to avoid glare and eyestrain. The best way is through proper general room illumination supplemented by task lighting from a lamp clamped to the far side of your drawing board. The lamps manufactured by Luxo are very commonly used. They combine excellent design for the purpose with reasonable cost. Any good reading or study lamp will do, however, if you are able to move it about as you need to. The great virtue of the Luxo lamps is that because of their long reach, several hinges and pivots, and counterbalanced design, they can be moved to light any area of the drawing surface and to eliminate glare.

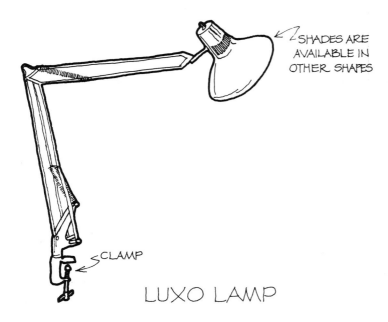

SHADES ARE AVAILABLE IN OTHER SHAPES

CLAMP

LUXO LAMP

T-SQUARE

The t-square enables you to draw lines that are consistently parallel to each other and perpendicular to the square edge of the drawing surface. The t-square you buy should preferably be 42″ long and not less than 36″. Its consistent parallelism depends on the straightness of the edge against which the t-square rides and upon the trueness (and tightness) of the joint between the head and the blade. Protect them! Don't let your t-square fall to the floor.

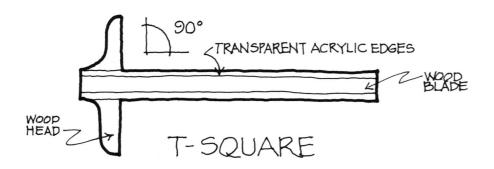

90°

TRANSPARENT ACRYLIC EDGES

WOOD BLADE

WOOD HEAD

T-SQUARE

PARALLEL STRAIGHTEDGES

The parallel straightedge, unlike the t-square, does not depend upon an edge of the drawing surface to maintain its parallelism, but rather rides on top of it. The parallel edge is guided by flexible, braided wires that run through it and along the sides of the board. Since the wires don't stretch, the straightedge rolls along them to positions up and down the board that are consistently parallel. The t-square will do the same, but the tightness of its head to the square edge of the board needs to be checked before you draw each line. Mayline makes the best parallel rules I know. They cost about three times as much as a t-square of comparable length. A t-square is essential for drawing perspectives, so if you buy a parallel straightedge, you will also eventually need a t-square.

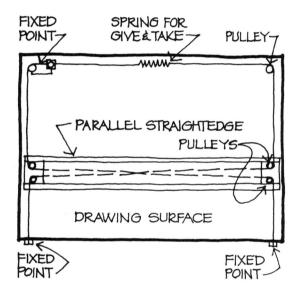

FIXED POINT

SPRING FOR GIVE & TAKE

PULLEY

PARALLEL STRAIGHTEDGE

PULLEYS

DRAWING SURFACE

FIXED POINT

FIXED POINT

THE BAR CAN MOVE UP AND DOWN THE BOARD AND STAY PARALLEL TO ITS FORMER POSITION(S) BECAUSE THE WIRES THAT CROSS OVER IN THE MIDDLE ARE OF CONSTANT LENGTH

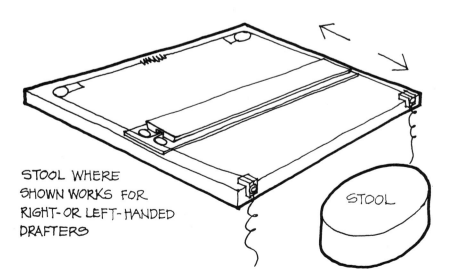

STOOL WHERE SHOWN WORKS FOR RIGHT- OR LEFT-HANDED DRAFTERS

STOOL

TRIANGLES

The next items you will need are triangles, which are used to guide your pencils or pens in drawing lines at any angle except parallel to the t-square or parallel edge. Certain drawing conventions we will discuss later make triangles that include angles of 30°-60°-90° and 45°-45°-90° the most useful, although an adjustable triangle can often be substituted for either. The latter is illustrated at the bottom of the page. You may eventually find, as I have, that one 18″ to 24″ 30°-60°-90° triangle for drawing borders and doing general layout, a 10″ or 12″ adjustable, and a small 4″ or 6″ 45° triangle are the most useful sizes to own. Triangles are measured along the back or left-hand vertical edge as drawn below.

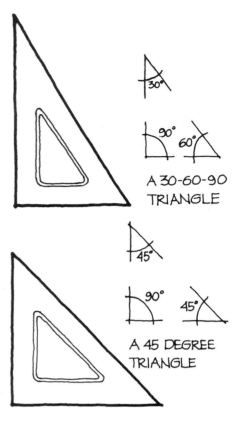

A 30-60-90 TRIANGLE

A 45 DEGREE TRIANGLE

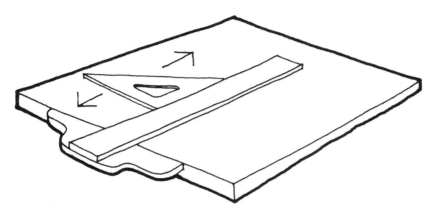

ADJUSTABLE TRIANGLES

For the past twenty years the triangle I have found myself using more than any other has been adjustable. Try out a friend's before you buy one—some people don't like them at all. The adjustable triangle is essentially a 45° triangle with its diagonal leg separable from the 90° L, pivoted at one end, and secured with a protractor bearing degree graduations. This allows the triangle to be set to any point over a range of 45°. Any of its three drawing edges can be placed against the blade of the t-square.

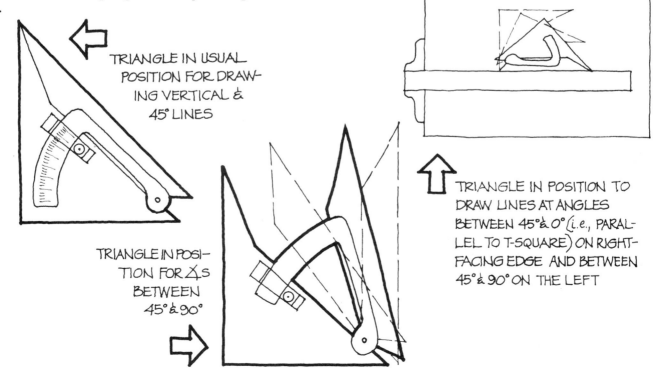

TRIANGLE IN USUAL POSITION FOR DRAWING VERTICAL & 45° LINES

TRIANGLE IN POSITION FOR ∡s BETWEEN 45° & 90°

TRIANGLE IN POSITION TO DRAW LINES AT ANGLES BETWEEN 45° & 0° (i.e., PARALLEL TO T-SQUARE) ON RIGHT-FACING EDGE AND BETWEEN 45° & 90° ON THE LEFT

PENCILS AND LEADS

To make lines against the straight edges provided by your t-square and triangles, you will need some sort of pencil. Two basic types are available: individual leads in reusable holders and drawing versions of the familiar yellow, wood-clinched writing pencil.

Regular pencils don't approach drawing leads for consistency. Drawing lead is compounded of a superfine graphite and clay mixture, smooth and free of impurities, which would chew up the drawing paper. Leads are graduated in numbered and lettered degrees. If a lead makes a line with light pressure, it is called "soft." If it requires a heavy touch to produce approximately the same line, it is "hard."

The wood-clinched pencils are difficult to use since the wood must be whittled away as shown before the lead can be sharpened.

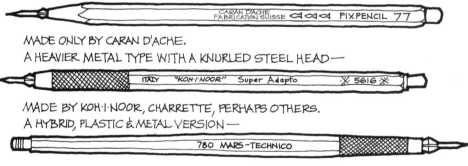

Don't sharpen these pencils in an ordinary pencil sharpener, because you'll get the wrong-shape point and you'll use them up much too fast (since drafting must always be done with a sharp lead).

Mechanical lead holders with a push-button lead-release mechanism come in three general types:

A LIGHT-WEIGHT TUBULAR ALUMINUM VERSION —

MADE ONLY BY CARAN D'ACHE.
A HEAVIER METAL TYPE WITH A KNURLED STEEL HEAD—

MADE BY KOH-I-NOOR, CHARRETTE, PERHAPS OTHERS.
A HYBRID, PLASTIC & METAL VERSION—

MADE BY STAEDTLER-MARS, EAGLE TURQUOISE, CHARRETTE.

Another thing you should know about drawing leads and pencils is that there are two basic types: those for drawing on conventional papers and boards and those for use on drawing films, known by the tradename "Mylar." Although the latter are generally used in offices, they are seldom used by students, since they are both expensive and provide an unnecessary degree of permanence. You will learn more about Mylar and leads to use on it as you progress through school and your professional career. So far as I have been able to ascertain, the leads used on Mylar that are closest in feel to those for regular use are made by Dixon.

PENCIL AND LEAD POINTERS

As they come from the factory leads have a short-taper point that must be immediately changed. If not you will find that the point blunts quickly, and you will have to interrupt your drawing to sharpen it then. A long-taper (about ⅜″) point (as described in Chapter 2) will retain its sharpness much longer and allow you to accomplish more before you need to repoint it. The objective of a lead pointer is to help you achieve the best taper for any given surface. You can also point your leads on a sandpaper block,

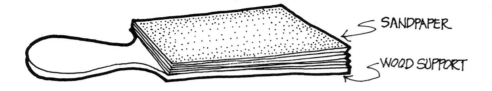

SANDPAPER

WOOD SUPPORT

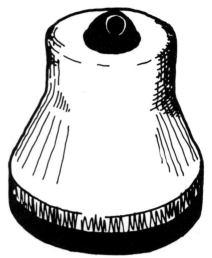

which takes some skill to use well, is messy, and is slower to use than a mechanical pointer. It also interrupts your drawing. I prefer to use a mechanical pointer made by Gedess (right).

It is light, fool-proof, durable and doesn't need to be clamped to a desk as many do. If you pack a kneadable eraser into its hollow bottom, once you've gotten your point, you can stab it into the eraser and clean off any lead shavings clinging to it. Other good pointers are made by Tru-Point, Boston, Mars-Technico. A good electric pointer is made by Behrens, though it is quite a luxury for beginners.

ERASERS

There are many erasers on the market, but only three you need know about to begin with. They are the Magic Rub by Faber-Castell, the Pink Pearl by Eberhard Faber, and whatever solvent-impregnated eraser your supplies dealer recommends for use with the ink you buy for the pens that will soon be described. Since erasing usually involves rubbing a paper surface in an effort to remove embedded graphite, there is a danger of damaging the paper fibers and altering the way the surface will take the next line. You must therefore always use the least abrasive eraser possible. The whole process is described in Chapter 2.

Use an erasing shield to limit the area being erased. Use a board brush to sweep eraser trailings off your board without smudging the remaining lines.

MAGIC-RUB

PINK PEARL

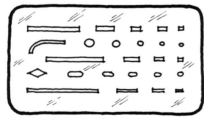

ERASING SHIELD
GET A SHIELD WITH SQUARE-
CORNERED CUTOUTS LIKE
THIS ONE FROM CHARRETTE

BOARD BRUSH

SCALES

Architects and designers use special rulers called "scales." With these rulers we are able to produce correctly proportioned drawings at reduced sizes *to a consistent ratio.* No interpretation of dimensions is needed to arrive at the reduced size; the scale is divided so that you can lay out drawings directly in feet and inches in reduced proportions. Each ruler usually has several sets of these scale ratios, which are individually also called scales, as, for example, ¼″ = 1′ scale. A scale of ¼″ means that each actual inch on the scale is subdivided into four equal parts, each representing one full-size foot. One of those parts at the end of the scale (it extends beyond the zero point) is usually subdivided into 6 or 12 parts representing inches to scale.

You will need at least two scales. One is an architect's scale, the other an engineer's. You will use the former to lay out most of your drawings, the latter to read engineering drawings and to lay out site plans. Both triangular and flat scales are popular. Each edge of a scale usually has two proportional scales superimposed on each other, as illustrated below.

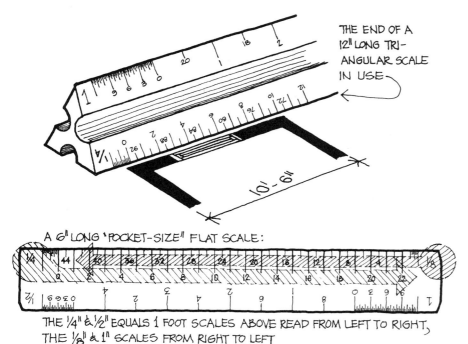

THE END OF A 12″ LONG TRI-ANGULAR SCALE IN USE

10′-6″

A 6″ LONG "POCKET-SIZE" FLAT SCALE:

THE ¼″ & ½″ EQUALS 1 FOOT SCALES ABOVE READ FROM LEFT TO RIGHT, THE ⅛″ & 1″ SCALES FROM RIGHT TO LEFT

TECHNICAL PENS

Since ink drawings are almost irresistible to students, who see them as a quick way to a professional-looking drawing, and since many teachers assign drawings in ink, we had best include a bit about technical pens. The type discussed here is the tubular-nib drafting pen. This is a pen of fixed line width manufactured in many versions, each of which makes a different width line. The pens are described by (and labeled with) their point diameters. They are sold singly and in families. The original of this type to achieve general acceptance was the Rapidograph technical fountain pen. A later, somewhat handier version is made with detachable point sections. A more recently introduced pen that I have used is the Faber-Castell TG.

It has a tiny sponge inside its cap that will, if it is kept wet, prevent ink from drying in the drawing tip (the nib).

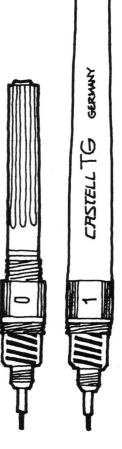

Yet a later generation of pen is represented by the Marsmatic 700 by Staedtler Mars. These pens have spring-loaded seals that push against the nibs and do what the sponge does in the Castell TGs. Rapidograph and Castell now also make pens with internal nib seals.

Point size (diameter) designations are handled differently by the various manufacturers for no apparent reason. There is a chart at the end of this section that correlates manufacturers' designations and actual diameters in millimeters.

The current versions of these pens are all about the same quality. If you decide you want to buy some or if you are required to use them for a course, it is worthwhile buying any of the three brands, depending on price. The pens are sometimes put on sale in sets just after the beginning of the school year. Hold out until then if you can.

Buy as large a set as you can afford. If you can swing it, I recommend a seven-pen set. Though these are expensive, the four-pen sets never seem to have an adequate range of point sizes to allow for expressive drawing.

METRIC SIZES	MARS	CASTELL	RAPIDOGRAPH
	5×0	4×0	6×0
.13mm	4×0	000	4×0
.18mm	3×0	00	3×0
.25mm	00		00
.30mm	0	0	0
.35mm			
.40mm		1	
.45mm	1		
.50mm	2	2	1
.60mm			2
.70mm	2½	2.5	2½
.80mm	3	3	3
1.0mm	3½	4	3½
1.2mm	4	5	4
1.4mm	5		6
2.0mm	6		7

PAPER AND TAPE

You should start your drawing with at least two types of paper. I won't recommend brands here: you should ask for samples (or buy small quantities) and test them for yourself. The paper types I recommend are:

1. A 20-pound tracing vellum 36″ wide by 20 yards long. This is an expensive, hard-finished, translucent rag paper to use for presentation drawings. Some vellums are formulated more for visual (optical) trans-

parency than for printing (technical) transparency. In choosing vellum, you must compromise between incompatible requirements and properties. For school use the paper with the greatest visual transparency is usually the best. These papers are made with plasticisers that degrade with age, causing the papers to become brittle, yellow, and loose their technical—or print—transparency. Such changes conflict with the needs of an office for both permanence and technical transparency, which explains why many other types of paper are made.

2. A very thin, fragile tissue paper usually 24″ wide by 50 yards long. This is a cheap, usually yellow but available in white or cream, tracing paper to use for design sketches and studies. It is often called "yellow-trace" or "canary."

If you can afford it, you should also invest in a detail paper. This is a nice paper for pencil or marker drawing. It is less translucent than some other vellums, but it is about 25 percent cheaper too. I do a lot of initial working-out on it and then trace the results onto the heavier vellums for the final drawings.

A gridded pad is useful for freehand sketches and early design studies. You can carry it with you when you make a survey of existing conditions (as you will learn to do in Chapter 3). These pads are available in both inexpensive and expensive papers. The most useful to a student is likely to be the inexpensive one.

You will need some drafting tape to secure the paper to your drawing surface while you draw. Drafting tape is a crepe paper tape much like masking tape, but it has a weaker adhesive that will not mark or leave a residue on your drawings.

I PREFER TO ORIENT MY TAPE THUS BECAUSE I FIND IT EASIER TO PULL THE PAPER OUT FLAT

OTHERS PREFER TO PLACE THE TAPE ACROSS THE CORNER, LIKE THIS

MARKERS

I depend heavily on markers for my presentation drawings. The ones I use come pre-inked and sealed. They are called Ad Markers, Magic Markers, Design Markers, and so on. These are the relatively inexpensive, relatively easy-to-use, modern equivalents of the watercolor washes architects were once famous for. Since the bulk of my drawing is black and white, it follows that most of my marker use is in the gray scale. Each maker manufactures a graduated series (1 through 10) of either warm or cool grays. I almost always use the warms. If you can afford it, get the full range; otherwise I recommend an abbreviated range—say, Warm 3 through Warm 8. Experiment: the grays don't look the same when used on the front as they do when used on the back of a translucent paper. They loose considerable density when you print them on diazo paper (that is, blue or black line paper) and gain density when photographed conventionally.

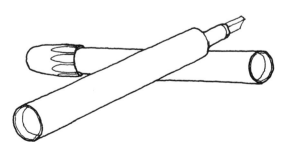

CHAPTER TWO

THE FIRST FEW LINES

Architects and designers draw with pencils. They also draw with technical pens and other exotica, but in the end they really draw with pencils. All the other line-making media are specialized: the pencil is what we think with. For this reason more than any other—and there are others— it is essential that you learn to draw with a pencil. Once you have mastered pencil technique, others are easier, and once you have learned to think and see in terms of pencil line, you will be able to translate your skills to other media.

For much presentation drawing the pencil is set against a straight edge, which can be a t-square or parallel rule or a triangle. The tools merely help you get straight lines. What you do with them and what you ultimately achieve is the result of thought and practice. How to use the tools to make those lines is the subject of this chapter.

The first few lines you make are often the hardest. The point is too sharp and breaks off. The little piece of lead that broke off, usually too small to notice, is large enough to make sweeping, curling scrawls on the drawing as you pass the straightedge over it. You make another point, blunt it slightly by scribbling a bit on a scratch pad so the above won't happen again, and set pencil to paper. This time you left too much of the lead exposed, and it breaks off where it enters the holder. You go through it all again, having learned the lessons of the previous experiences. This time you succeed and make a line. You sit back to examine it and discover when you move the straightedge away that your line wanders up and down the page like an ocean swell, and its weight (thickness as well as "blackness") changes within its length.

These things have all happened to me, and some still do when I use a new paper or surface. That should be a clue to you: there are many variables in this game, and all of us must explore them. If the paper is more resistant to the passage of the lead or if the lead is less willing to be ground away by the surface of the paper, the whole feel of the procedure will be different from what you are used to. For this reason it is sensible at the beginning of your learning to standardize on as few products as possible—eliminate as many variables as you can! And then you must practice.

DRAFTING LINES

A reasonable early exercise is to draw lines—any lines—using your new tools. The lines don't need a meaning—just draw. A demonstration is helpful here, so follow the drawings and words carefully:

1. Always keep a "sharpish" point on your lead (see what that means below).

2. Always tuck the point of your lead against the t-square or triangle you are using (this prevents the point—and line—from wandering), and always pull the lead along the edge—don't push it.

3. Always hold down the edge against which you are drawing. If you tuck the lead against that edge without holding it down, it will tend to lift, so hold it down.

4. Rotate the lead holder or pencil as you make lines. This will ensure that a new lead surface is in contact with the paper at each point along your line and will wear away the lead evenly. This technique will help you make uniform lines and will keep your point usable longer.

5. Swing your arm from the shoulder. Don't let your hand or forearm drag on the paper or straightedge.

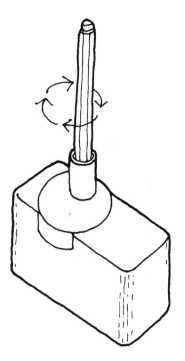

Here's what those five points mean in detail:

1. A sharp point will produce a clean, dark, sharp-edged line. If the point becomes blunt, the line will lose its sharpness and "gray-out," since the point will lay down the same amount of graphite over a wider contact area with the same hand pressure. To vary the blackness of your lines, use different grades of lead. See the Pencils and Leads section in Chapter 1 and below.

The leads and pencils we use all have a point as they come from the factory. It must be modified, since its taper is incorrect. Your first job, once you have inserted the lead in the holder, is to sharpen it to the right taper. To sharpen a lead you must: extend about ¾" of lead from the bottom of the lead-holder chuck. Put the lead-and-holder combination in the pointer, and rotate it gently. The type of rotation depends on the type of pointer; see below. The lead is ground away inside the pointer by an abrasive or a cutting wheel. The amount of drag you will feel as the lead is ground away varies with the hardness of the lead. Soft leads, and especially waxy, colored leads, cling to the cutting wheel and break off easily in the pointer. Hard leads, on the other hand, are brittle, and will also break off in the pointer if you handle them roughly or try to sharpen them too rapidly. Go easy.

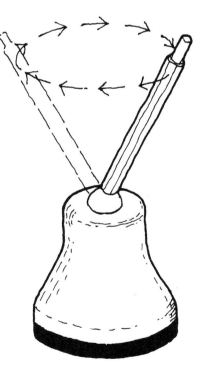

The right taper varies from job to job and paper to paper. It is simply that angle which compromises the longest wearing point (that is, the skinniest) with the one least likely to break (the bluntest). Since each paper (and even each batch of paper) has a different tooth, or resistance to the passage of the pencil over it, the breaking point of any given lead will depend at least in part on the paper it is dragged over. A good idea of the kind of taper to strive for is given in the enlarged sketches below. *Important reservation:* A sharp point is a relative thing. If your lead pointer is working well, the points it produces will look like this (much enlarged):

NEEDLE POINT

What you want is something that looks like this:

JUST RIGHT!

That doesn't mean this!

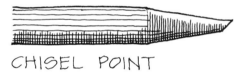

CHISEL POINT

Or this!

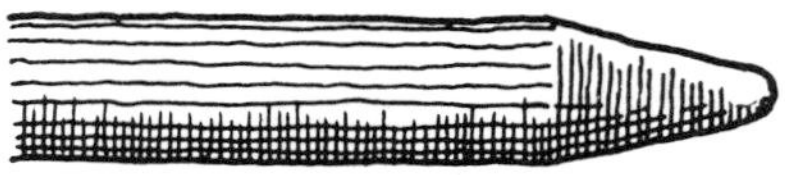

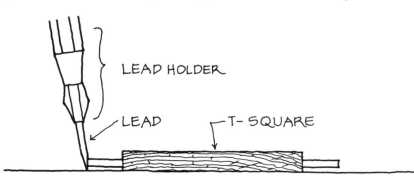

TOO DULL!

After pointing with the pointer, scribble lightly and briefly on a piece of scrap paper while turning the lead and holder. This will give you just the right amount of bluntness to draw with and will help prevent the point from breaking as described above.

2. I always try to keep the point of my pencil against the lower corner of my drawing edge (as seen here), whether it is a triangle or a t-square. If you examine the drawing below, you will understand why:

LEAD HOLDER

LEAD   T-SQUARE

If the point is tucked in to the edge, then the line it makes when moved along that edge will be as straight and smooth as the edge. It is almost impossible to maintain a straight line by muscle tension alone, which is what you would have to do if you relied on the setup shown here:

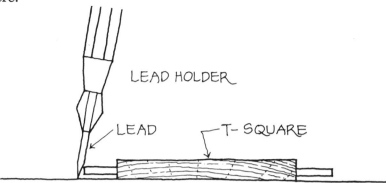

LEAD HOLDER

LEAD   T-SQUARE

This allows the lead to pivot back and forth (and causes the line to waver like an ocean swell) around the top corner of the drawing edge.

Always keep your hand (and the upper end of the pencil) ahead of the lead tip as you make lines. In other words, always *pull* the lead along the paper. Don't *push*—the tip will dig in and ruin your drawing.

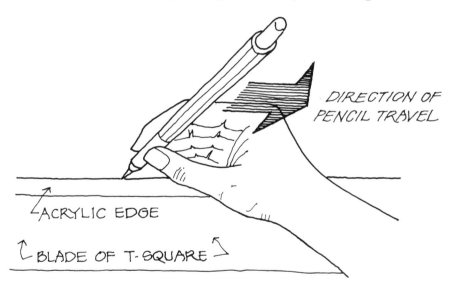

DIRECTION OF PENCIL TRAVEL

ACRYLIC EDGE

BLADE OF T-SQUARE

If you are right-handed, you should make your horizontal lines by pulling the lead from left to right. If you are left-handed, pull from right to left, and do not try to imitate the methods of a righty unless you have reason to believe that you are ambidextrous.

3. One hand holds the pencil, the other holds down the edge being drawn against. Always. Both hands move: the one with the pencil to make the line, the other to assist the first in functioning well. The latter is also used to check the position of the t-square's head in relation to the board edge before you make each line. *Always.* If you are using a parallel rule and you are confident that it is set up right (that is, with the wire clamped tight in the adjusting clamp), then each position you place it in will be parallel to the ones before. You won't need to check each horizontal line as you do the t-square, but you will need to do the following in either case. Before you make a vertical or inclined line, always check the position of the triangle to make sure it is seated flat on the t-square or parallel rule.

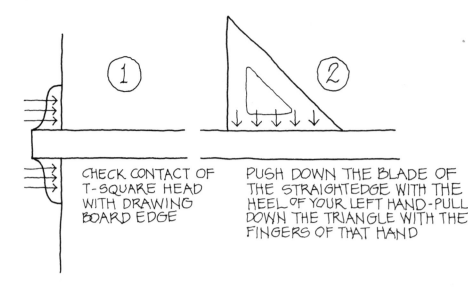

① CHECK CONTACT OF T-SQUARE HEAD WITH DRAWING BOARD EDGE

② PUSH DOWN THE BLADE OF THE STRAIGHTEDGE WITH THE HEEL OF YOUR LEFT HAND—PULL DOWN THE TRIANGLE WITH THE FINGERS OF THAT HAND

This illustration shows the t-square-to-triangle relationship for making vertical lines that is used by a right-handed person. The left hand pulls down the triangle to the t-square. The right arm wraps over and around the left hand and triangle and starts the new vertical line at the bottom of the triangle's vertical edge. The lined is *pulled* up toward the top of that vertical edge.

A setup for making vertical lines for left-handed drafters

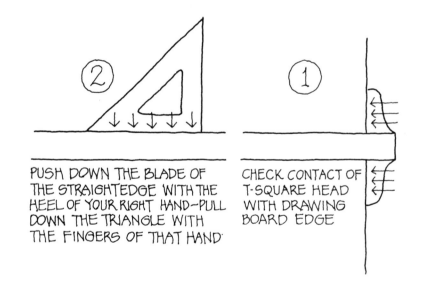

② PUSH DOWN THE BLADE OF THE STRAIGHTEDGE WITH THE HEEL OF YOUR RIGHT HAND—PULL DOWN THE TRIANGLE WITH THE FINGERS OF THAT HAND·

① CHECK CONTACT OF T-SQUARE HEAD WITH DRAWING BOARD EDGE

is a mirror image of the right-handed setup just shown. Here the triangle is pulled down onto the t-square by the right hand, and the left, holding the pencil, wraps over it and the triangle and makes the line, again *pulling* from the bottom to the top of the triangle.

4. The rotation called for is possibly the hardest thing to learn in this chapter. The illustrations show start and end hand positions, but the hard part is coordinating the rotation while keeping the point tucked in to the edge. The idea is to roll the pencil between your thumb and first finger. The thumb pushes forward while the finger curls inward toward the palm: it is the same motion you use to wind up a pocket or wrist watch or the strands of a thread or fishline if they start to come undone. Only practice can help you here. It's a motion that doesn't come naturally, but must be learned.

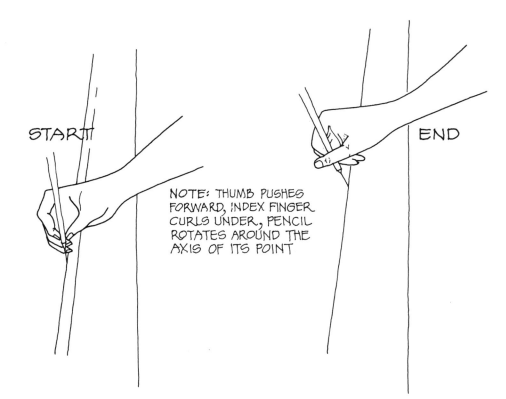

START

END

NOTE: THUMB PUSHES FORWARD, INDEX FINGER CURLS UNDER, PENCIL ROTATES AROUND THE AXIS OF ITS POINT

5. To understand this point, you need to think about what you are doing. We are all accustomed to writing letters and the like, and for such small projects we have gotten used to resting the heels of our hands on the writing surface—or on the paper itself. But this drawing we are working on now is no small project; it is an undertaking with long lines and large gestures that require bold, sustained, sweeping movements. These are made by the whole arm, which is a remarkable device designed for just such uses. Swing your arm from the shoulder! Use your long muscles to control that puny pencil! Don't try to make long lines by finger movements alone. You'll get short, choppy line segments that may join at the ends, but don't make a unified whole.

Now let's discuss lead or pencil grades and paper and erasures.

LEADS

The lead makes the line, and line is the paramount thing in drawing. There are many leads (see Chapter 1 for a description of how the grades work in relation to feel), and the choice of which to use is puzzling. Take heart—the leads you will need cover a fairly narrow range, and all the others are for special purposes. We'll get to some of them, but be assured: with no more than three or four different grades you can explore pencil technique.

The leads that cluster around the middle of the range are the ones most people use most of the time. In a working day I use H, 2H, 4H, and sometimes F leads—when I'm working with holders and conventional, 2-mm diameter, leads. This is a fairly hard range, but then I really bear down, with all the attendant problems described below under Erasing. When I am working with thin-lead holders (the .5-mm diameter is the type I have), I use B, HB, H, and 2H. Remember when you start your drawing to select as soft a lead as you can possibly work with. A good starting range is the softer one described above—B, HB, H, 2H. The softer leads have the following advantages:

1. They make a darker line with less effort and consequently less fatigue.

2. They do less damage to the paper as you press down to make your line, with benefits described below.

3. They are less brittle than the harder leads and are therefore less likely to break.

But they smear. Therein lies the paradox confronted by all of us: the appropriate lead for a given situation is always a compromise among ease of use, durability of point, and personal requirements including feel and working style.

It is essential, if you will be working with soft leads, that you be neat. Clean your tools often. Start at the top of your paper and work down. Don't rub the heel of your hand over the lines you have made. If you think you will be working the drawing over and over, go to a paper with a harder finish and to a harder lead. Cover completed portions of the drawing with a clean piece of yellow trace.

You will do a lot of erasing. The process of designing involves trial and error, so erasing becomes a positive thing, representing the development of an idea. Let go of the association of erasing with mistakes, since it really doesn't apply here.

Before we can talk about erasing, however, we need a word about paper, which interacts powerfully with both the drawing and the erasing.

PAPERS

In the early stages of designing you will find yourself using the cheapest of all papers, usually referred to as "yellow trace." It won't withstand erasures, since it tears very easily. (It is also called "flimsy.") The whole point of it is to be transparent in both the visual and intellectual sense, which means that you shouldn't try to erase on it. Rather, tear off the piece you are working on, unroll some new over it, and sketch your new ideas. If you stop to erase on it, you will break the flow of your thinking and become enmeshed in technique, since erasing on yellow trace takes lots of care and attention. My advice: don't do it—yellow trace is for ideas. The best media for these quick sketches are fine-line markers (Pilot Razor Point, Niji Stylist, for example) and soft, fat-lead pencils such as Eagle 314 Draughting and Eberhard Faber Ebony.

As you move up the scale of drawing refinement, you will doubtless want a different paper, one on which you can lavish some skill and effort, with a reasonable expectation that the drawing will survive the process. This means, among other things, a paper that can withstand erasures. I use one called Clearprint 1000H for this stage.

I like to work things out on 1000H (also called a "detail" paper) because it is a rather white, relatively opaque paper. Lines stand out on it in bold contrast, which makes tracing whatever is worked out on it onto a "final" or presentation drawing quite easy. I almost never present on 1000H, unless I want an "interim," in-process, look.

Though 1000H is versatile, I find that quick sketches look a little forlorn on it. It is a paper that seems to demand greater precision than yellow trace does. Detail paper really is best for working things out and takes to drafted pencil line better than any other paper I know. It handles ink drawing equally well.

For presentation drawings I use a French vellum widely distributed in this country called Vidalon, made by Canson & Montgolfier. It is a classic

European vellum, with great visual transparency. It resembles parchment (to a degree) and yields beautiful drawings. Unlike Clearprint, Vidalon is so translucent it looks gray unless backed by a reflecting white surface. It takes pencil, ink, and colored pencil lines well. It has very substantial tooth, which means you need to sharpen your pencils often. If instead you go to a harder lead, the paper will groove where you draw and leave a ghost when you erase. Drawbacks of the paper (aside from the foregoing) are that it yellows and becomes brittle with age and cracks easily along a fold line.

To back up presentation drawings on Vidalon, I usually use a white-faced Bristol board.

Many other vellums exist, formulated to satisfy different needs. A paper with good technical transparency (for easy printing) is Charrette's 916H. It is significantly harder to trace on than the Vidalon (since it is less visually transparent) and seems to hold up better over time.

ERASING

Erasing is really the process of lifting a line. The best erasure is the one that pulls the graphite away from (or out of) the paper fibers with the least damage to them. "Rubbing it out" is precisely what I don't mean—more likely you will rub it in. What's called for here is a combination of the appropriate eraser and a light touch. You need to apply the eraser in a sort of flicking or scooping motion. Edges of the rubber contact edges of the graphite particles that form the line you want erased and lift them from the surface. In the process, the eraser crumbles, which works to your benefit, since it means that the eraser in contact with your good, expensive paper is always clean.

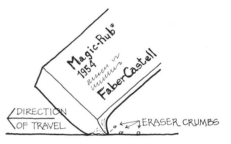

I'm describing the ideal. Typically, the graphite is "burned" into the paper and won't come out. Or if it does, it leaves what's called a "ghost." This happens for one or two reasons: you bore down too hard on the pencil when you were making the line in the first place, or you used too hard a lead for the purpose. In either case you have cut a groove in the paper and lined its sides with graphite forcefully applied. There isn't much to do about it this time. Remember when you set out to draw to select as soft a lead as you can possibly work with and to go to a yet softer lead when you want to make the darkest lines. Bearing down on the pencil just means you run the risk of breaking off the point (very easy to do) and prevents you from being able to erase the lines you no longer want.

Now when you do erase, you must use the softest (most friable or easily crumbled) eraser you own that will also do the job. The first of the recommended erasers in Chapter 1, the Magic-Rub, is made of air-entrapped plastic or synthetic rubber. The eraser crumbles as the trapped air bubbles come under the pressure of the rubbing and presents sharp (if soft) edges to the line and paper. Result: effective erasing, little damage to the paper. But what if some of what you were erasing is left behind? Try the Pink Pearl. This is a much coarser eraser, so be gentle. If it fails, try a Ruby by Eberhard Faber, which is really an old-fashioned, abrasive ink eraser.

Both of these erasers will roughen the paper surface where you have been rubbing, and the roughness they create will affect the way the paper takes your line-making media. Of these, pencil is least affected by variations in the paper surface, ink and marker most. Do practice a flicking or lifting motion for your erasing; it will cause the least damage to the paper.

PRACTICE YOUR LINES

Now that we've covered all aspects of line making and removal, let's get in some practice. Make a whole series of lines starting at the top of the paper and moving down the page. Practice sharpening your pencil or lead. Rotate the pencil or holder as you go along the line. Stop and inspect each one. Slide the t-square or parallel rule up to the line you've just made, and cast your eye along it. Is it really straight? Or does it wander a little? If it does, practice tucking the point in to the edge of the t-square or parallel rule. Does it fatten out very quickly along its length?

LINES BEGIN NARROW, FLARE WIDE. PENCIL NOT ROTATED

If it does, you need to either: use a harder lead, or work on that pencil rotation (or both). Keep at it—fill the page.

Get out a triangle (I suggest the adjustable one), and make a series of vertical lines. Inspect each line. If any wander, work on holding down the triangle with the heel of your hand.

CORNERS

Now let's try some corners. There are really only two acceptable ways to represent a corner, or intersection of two nonparallel lines. They are to make them meet perfectly or to overshoot. Since I seem always to be in a hurry, I find it simplest to let the lines overshoot. The overshot makes the corner look crisp and definitely telegraphs to the viewer that the lines *meet*. An undershot corner always looks rounded off, and to someone viewing the drawing from a distance, it seems *intended* to be a rounded corner.

How much overshoot is enough, and how much is too much? The answer varies with the drawing, but more than 1/8″ will start to look sloppy.

INK DRAWING

Eventually you will want to try drawing in ink. Some tricks will help make the experience less painful.

Any discussion of pens is complicated (for me at least) by the fact that good ink drawing is highly sophisticated, exacting, and slow. It is therefore appropriate to quite refined, developed design presentations, and not to most school situations. I further believe that design students should first master pencil techniques. The pens produce such a "cool," demanding line that errors of judgment and control are very apparent. It takes experience to produce drawings in ink that exhibit both richness and control. Pencil drawing is somewhat more forgiving. Nonetheless, whole schools seem to pursue that elusive good ink drawing.

To begin, fill only those pens you plan to experiment with; no one has yet figured out a way to make technical pens easy to clean. Fill the pens with the ink their manufacturer included with them. You may eventually decide that there are meaningful differences among various brands of ink, but for now it is simplest to use the type supplied by the pens' own maker. Fill the pens precisely as the manufacturer instructs you.

Tubular nib drawing pens are all basically the same. A tube delivers ink directly to the drawing surface. The width of the line made is determined by the outside diameter of the point and is designated on the pen in several places. The flow of ink is regulated by a plunger attached to a thin wire that runs down through the tube and extends a fraction of a millimeter beyond it. When you place nib to paper, the wire is pushed up into the tube, which in turn allows the ink to flow. These mechanisms are delicate and need a gentle touch.

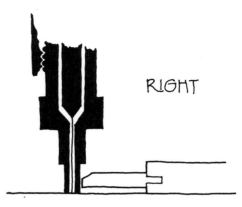

When you are ready to begin, take one of the pens (with the cap off) and place the nib down gently on your paper. The pens must be held at right angles to the drawing surface to work properly. Straight up and down. They will then give you a line of accurate and constant width. If you tip them more than a few degrees, the ink will flow out through capillary action and blob more ink onto the paper at the high side than you want, giving you uneven line widths.

If the pen makes a mark this first time, then consider yourself lucky and continue making both drafted and freehand lines with it. Try out its maneuverability, like a car's. These pens are not good for all uses or for all papers—they are designed for drafting lines while being held against a straightedge. So long as you hold them upright, you can make consistent lines. You can use them for freehand tracing of previously drafted lines and get a "freehand" presentation. But they won't work for sketching, since they don't have the flexibility to follow a calligraphic motion.

If the pen doesn't make a line—the ink isn't yet flowing—hold it over a piece of scrap paper and shake it up and down the way you would a salt shaker if you were using it on a humid summer's day (because the holes were clogged) and you really loved salt. Don't hit the drawing board. Try it again. And again. When it finally works, proceed as above.

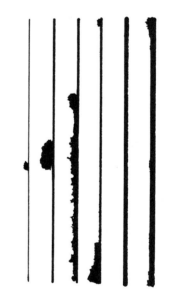

So long as you make horizontal lines against your t-square or parallel rule, you can be an expert. These tools are made so that they work very readily with ink pens. Not so your triangles. Sooner or later as you draw vertical lines, you run into difficulty. Typically, you draw a line, remove the triangle to have a look, and discover, to your horror, something that looks like this.

The cause is capillary action: the ink is drawn into the very narrow space between the paper and the triangle and forms as large a blot as there is ink to make. The drawing is ruined, or at least your production schedule is set back by the time needed to get rid of the blot, so it is best to learn early on how to avoid these accidents.

Since the problem is caused by capillary action, the easiest solution is to raise the triangle so that there is no capillary space.

One way to do this is to put tape on the underside of your triangle. A problem with this is that the tape, if left on a long time, bonds chemically with the plastic and won't come off. Later, when it gets really dirty, you have a ruined triangle. I prefer, therefore, to raise my triangles up off the paper surface with a shim. My shim is a circle template, which is perfect for this secondary use. Some people glue pennies or dimes to the undersides of their triangles to lift them. Any thin plastic stock will do, or you can hunt around for cast triangles that have an undercut edge. These are generally less accurate than ordinary triangles, which are cut from acrylic sheet. Because they are less accurate, they are less popular than the cut variety and are therefore less widely available. If you find one that is accurate, buy it and take care of it—it might last you twenty years or more!

INK ERASING

Ink is a permanent medium. The paradox of removing a permanent medium has plagued drafters for as long as they've existed, and attempts at a solution have involved everything from Fiberglas brushes that left slivers in your fingers (and ruined the drawing surface) to razor blades that left your fingers in slivers.

Mylar drawing films have solved much of the problem, though not for students who seldom use them. Erasing ink on Mylar involves nothing more than wetting a clean portion of your MagicRub eraser and washing off the line. Use an erasing shield to limit the area washed.

The recent introduction of solvent-impregnated erasers has been a boon to students. These erasers really work, though you must observe a few ground rules. Buy the eraser made by the manufacturer of the ink you use or one recommended for it. Buy a new eraser before you begin a new set of presentation drawings. The solvent evaporates after a fairly short while, and an old eraser is useless. Expect to rub a lot with these erasers. Their effect is cumulative, and the lines you are removing won't disappear right away. Carefully brush the eraser shavings from your drawing. They are saturated with solvent and will take part of what you want to keep with them if you are brusque.

CLEANING PENS—OR THE WORST IS LAST

Technical pens need to be cleaned. India ink is really a suspension of minute solids, and if allowed to dry, it will clog up your pens so they are unusable. The manufacturers show you how to clean their pens and give you explicit warnings about what will happen if you take them apart further than recommended. Practically, I find that the manufacturer's recommendations don't get the pens clean. The water doesn't penetrate far enough into the fine recesses to displace the ink. Eventually it dries out, and the points must be discarded. I take my points apart, clean them under running water, dry them fully, and reassemble carefully. The part to be extra careful replacing is the inner weight and feeler wire. In the smaller point sizes the feeler wire is very thin and can easily crumple if you reinsert it into the tubular part without care. If you do crumple it you will need to replace the point, since spare feeler wires aren't made.

Be sure your pens are dry before you close them up and put them away. Modern pens have excellent seals that keep the ink moist longer. Unfortunately, these seals also keep any stray water inside longer, and your points will corrode if kept wet (except by ink).

Use cool water to clean them.

Remember that the stuff you are washing off is India ink and that it will ruin any porous surface it splashes onto.

GENERAL CLEANUP

While we're on the subject of cleaning things, we might as well look at the general subject. Graphite is dirty. It is compounded (in pencil leads) to stick. It sticks. The proper way to use it is by rubbing it up against the tools you use to draw with, which are mostly made of acrylic plastic because they need to be transparent. The graphite makes them dirty and less transparent. Worse, it is carried by the tools to the paper's surface and is there deposited in minute though significant quantities. By the time your drawing is complete, the formerly white paper has taken on a dull gray cast. Your carefully drafted lines no longer stand out in bold contrast. The drawing is diminished. Moral: wash your tools often with plain soap and water. Dry them thoroughly with terry-cloth towels or flannel. When they get gummed up, try rubber cement thinner (which is flammable) or an adhesive remover. It's hard to find, but does the job.

After using any solvent, wash the tools. The solvents are usually petroleum-based and leave an oily residue, which will ruin your paper.

CHAPTER THREE

BASIC DRAWINGS

There are conventions in design drawing just as there are in driving an automobile or most other human endeavors. These conventions are properly regarded as positive benefits: it is not necessary for us to invent drawing types every time we have a three-dimensional idea to share. The conventions also mean that the greatest number of our viewers—at least among the design professions and also among some of the general population—will be prepared to understand what they look at. Conventions in this sense are vocabularies; they are conventions of understanding.

The basic drawings usually required to present a design are the plan, section, and elevation. These three views have been used by designers since the Renaissance to describe the products of their imaginations. The three dimensions of reality are described by them, and a volumetric idea of the object is conveyed. Of course, these are very stereotyped drawings, locked in by the same conventions. What the general public needs in the way of drawings to be able to understand a designer's ideas may be quite different from what other designers might need, so the issue of presentation goes further than conventions. Other views more congenial to that general public, such as perspectives, are the subject of several later chapters in this book.

For now it is enough to start with the three basic views. The other drawings in fact are constructed on the bones of these base drawings, which must therefore come first.

THE PLAN

The plan drawing—possibly the most familiar of all architectural drawings—must be clearly thought about and understood. Though this drawing is frequently referred to as a "floor plan," it in fact represents a horizontal cut through the building or space at windowsill height. All material above the cut (with a few minor exceptions—see below) is considered to be discarded, and the designer is thereby

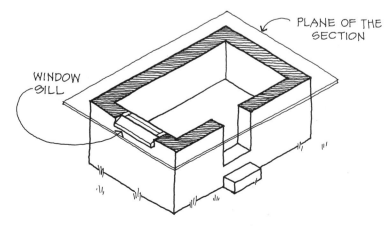

PLANE OF THE SECTION

WINDOW SILL

able to look directly down into the "pan" that remains—that is, the floor surrounded by 2- to 3-foot high stub walls.

The plan is drawn as though the eye of the designer were directly above every point in the drawing—a condition only possible through levitation—and looking straight down (the line of sight is at right angles to the surface of the floor). In the case of presentation drawings the walls are pochéd (darkened in) where they have been cut through by the horizontal section to indicate that they are "felt" to be solid.

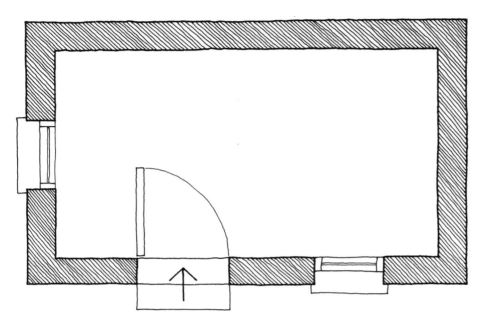

THE VERTICAL SECTION

The next drawing in the initial triad is also a section, but the cut this time is in the vertical plane. Once again whatever is "behind" the cut is discarded, and we are able to look directly into the building. This is a lot like looking into a doll's house—everything is revealed in miniature.

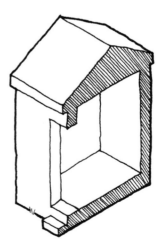

The section is inextricably linked to the plan and to the designing of volumes. It is developed at the same time as the plan—not afterwards! Coupled with a plan or plans, it helps the viewer understand the volumetric intentions of the designer. It gives a great deal of information about the qualities of a space and the heights of sills and other mundane pieces of building shown on the plans.

THE ELEVATION

The final drawing of the triad is the elevation. It does not represent a section or slice, as the other two do, but rather depicts the facade or facades of a building or object (including interior elevations) as though the designer were suspended directly in front of each element and at right angles to the principal plane of the drawing. Think of Peter Pan or of hummingbirds here, able to dart about to each part of the subject and examine it head on.

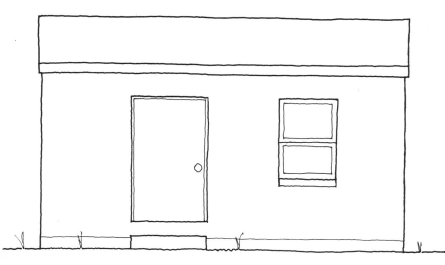

ORTHOGRAPHIC PROJECTIONS

Drawing emerged as a field of serious study in the Renaissance. The ability to accurately record the world, in perspective and other drawings, was widely expected to increase knowledge of its scientific basis. Accordingly, study of drawing was regarded as scientific research. Among other things, drawings were classified by type. In Renaissance science it was believed that images on the retinas of our eyes are made by rays emanating from the object seen. Though this is fanciful, it is not so far from what we know to be true: images to our eyes are drawn by rays of light reflected by the object seen. The classification system used in the Renaissance had antecedents in Greek geometry. Orthographic drawings—the word "orthography" has roots in Greek that mean "right drawing"—are made by rays that meet the paper *only at right angles*. These drawings provide flat, true-to-scale images of the object drawn. Such views are seldom seen in nature except of very small objects.

The plan, section, and elevation drawings we have just studied are popularly referred to as orthographic projections. There are more drawings—including axonometrics, which we will study—that are orthographic. Even though the orthographic category contains other drawing types, people generally understand you to mean plan, section, elevation when you refer to orthographic drawings or projections.

The second large category of drawings includes those made by rays that meet the drawing paper at angles other than 90°—obliques. The most familiar of these are perspectives, which we will also study.

The easiest way to understand the three basic views (and those that follow) is to make some of them of a familiar space. What I ask my students to do is draw their own rooms or apartments for this exercise and layer new information onto their drawings as their knowledge grows. In this way they conclude their studies with me with a coordinated set of presentation drawings of one place.

A MEASURED SURVEY

Before you can make a drafted plan of your home, you must start with a measured survey. Sections and elevations are constructed from the plan and a few other pieces of data. The survey begins it all. Start it by sketching a plan. You don't need to be dimensionally accurate—just try for something that resembles the layout of your place.

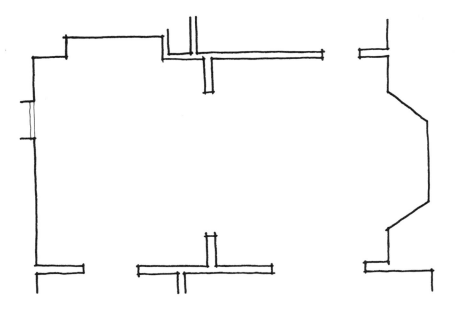

Remember that interior walls have thickness (usually 4½″ to 6″) and allow for it. Exterior walls do too, usually 10½″ to 12″ if brick or stone, about 6″ to 9″ if wood. We'll check these dimensions later. Remember also that your layout is made at windowsill height and show all openings. What do you do if there is a high window in your place (as, for example, in a bathroom)? Show it too; these conventions are meant to be helpful, not iron-bound. The exact height of the windowsills will be shown in the elevations or sections in any case.

Now take a tape measure, and starting in one corner of a room, work your way around its four (or more) sides in sequence, measuring and recording horizontal distances. It is easiest to make a survey with a friend who can hold the end of the tape, which must be kept taut. You need to be consistent here: measure all the windows and doors to the same part of their frames (see below). Note all your measurements on your sketched plan in a consistent way. When you draw up this survey later, you will need as much clarity as possible. If you want to check on the parallelism of the room, measure the two diagonals. If they are within an inch or so, you have a very square room (not square in plan, square at the corners).

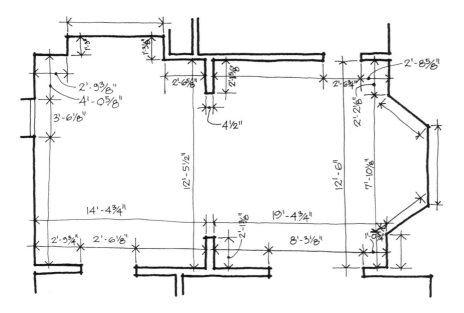

WALL THICKNESSES

The thickness of a wall is revealed at the openings in it. A little understanding of construction techniques here will help you uncover the facts. Most walls in residential construction are made of vertical "sticks"—properly called "studs" (which may be wood or metal)—with nominal dimensions of either 2″ × 4″ or 2″ × 6″. In a typical wall these are placed with their biggest dimension at right angles to the plane of the wall (this makes it stiff). Plaster is attached to both sides of the studs. The plaster may have been applied wet—in an older house—over thin strips of wood nailed to the studs and called "lath," or it may be in the form of plasterboard, more properly called "gypsum wallboard," nailed directly to the studs.

In either case, where the stud and plaster assembly reaches an opening, the edge is covered by an opening liner, usually made of wood. Trim is attached to both edges of the liner, but usually set back a bit from the opening. It overlaps both the liner and the plaster and conceals their join. Thus it is possible to measure the liner width and thereby the width (or thickness) of the wall. Look at the drawing, and look at your doors.

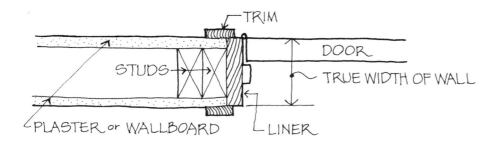

For windows the convention is to measure their widths to the points on either side where the wall changes direction by 90° and heads away from the observer and toward the window itself, that is, the wall opening. If the wall is very thin and the window and its liner fill the thickness of the wall, then measure to the liner—*not* to the pieces that hold the moving parts of the window (called the "sash") in place, which are technically known as the "stops."

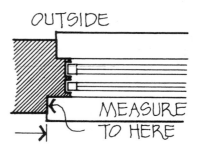

35

MEASURED PLANS

Now that you have a complete survey it is time to start making a measured plan. Decide on a scale to use. This is related to the size of your apartment (if you dwell in marble halls, use $1/16'' = 1'$; if more modest, then $1/4'' = 1'$ will do); to the size of the paper you have—if you have a 20' long space, at $1/4'' = 1'$ the drawing will require 5'' of paper, plus white space around it; to the size of your equipment and workspace; and to the amount of detailed information you plan to show on the drawings. In general, the more detail the larger the scale should be to allow room for the detail to be read and understood. For this exercise, $1/4'' = 1'$ is the preferred scale, although if your place is small, you may wish to draw it at $1/2'' = 1'$.

LAYOUT LINES

The first thing you will draw is layout lines. These are very faint construction lines that have no direct role to play in the final drawing, but that enable you to locate things from your survey on your final drawing before you are ready to burn them in with a dark, black line. They are traditionally made with a hard lead—4H or even harder—to prevent any substantial mark. The harder leads take a finer point and therefore make a thinner, more accurate mark, which is useful when you are laying out a long string of short dimensions. The final product will be more accurate. Some people use no-print blue pencils for their layouts. I don't like them for this because their leads are soft and waxy and inherently inaccurate. If you don't have a 4H lead, then use a 2H with a very light touch. Keep the point sharp!

Now, lay a fresh piece of "working-out" paper on your board as shown in Chapter 1. I use 1000H Clearprint for this. Draw a baseline below which you do not want the drawing to go. This point is usually 3'' or 4'' above the bottom edge of the drafting surface, though it can be more. Again, this is related to several factors, including the ultimate size of the drawing, the size of your belly, the length of your reach, and so on.

It is important to position both the paper and the drawing on the paper so that you have to reach as little as possible. Reaching is fatiguing, and a tired drafter makes mistakes. Now, near the left edge of the paper (or the right edge if you are left-handed), make a long vertical line with your biggest triangle, beyond which you do not want the drawing to extend. You have established the lower left corner of your drawing and can start laying out the measured plan based on the dimensions taken during your survey.

LAYING OUT A MEASURED PLAN

The simplest way to set up a drawing is to lay out a "string" of dimensions all at once. A string is a series of measurements along a line. Here is where you will begin to appreciate the design of the architect's scale, since you will be able to directly transpose the dimensions on your survey to proportional dimensions on your drawing without doing any figuring. If the room measured 19' 5'' wide, then put your scale on the paper so that the space between the 4'' and 6'' gradations on the subdivided end of the scale is on your reference mark (presumably, the line that represents the wall you originally measured from).

Now go along the scale until you come to 19' and make a light tick mark on the paper directly below the 19' mark with either your no-print or your 4H pencil. Now shift the scale so that 0'' is over the tick mark you just made. Measure along the inch gradations until you come to $4\frac{1}{2}''$ (or whatever thickness is appropriate to the walls in your place), and make another mark. You have now laid out the wall between one room and the next. Lay out the width of the next room. Continue until you have laid out the entire string of dimensions in the direction you started in. Now lay out the string that runs at right angles to the one you just completed. If you have a complex space to draw, full of corner columns and ins-and-outs, you may find it easier to lightly draft the whole line at each point rather than just make a tick mark. If you do you will end up with a ghostly outline of your final drawing.

Now go back and lay in the shorter dimensions—the positions of doors and windows, of columns, of any local eccentricities such as pilasters or recesses in the walls. When you have everything that is part of the building's intrinsic structure in your drawing, step back and have a cup of coffee before continuing.

At this point I like to draw in everything lightly if I haven't already done so. This doesn't take long, since the tick marks are there, and I become familiar with the lines of the whole drawing. That helps in the next step.

What we do next is more mechanical and less thoughtful than the preceeding work, but nonetheless requires attention and judgment. Every line laid out or implied by ticked dimensions must be "heavied up." To do this you need a softer lead than you have been working with. I suggest an H or an F. Since the softer leads smear easily, I like to start this process in the upper-left corner of the drawing (I'm right-handed) and work down and away from it. That way I am less likely to smudge what I've completed.

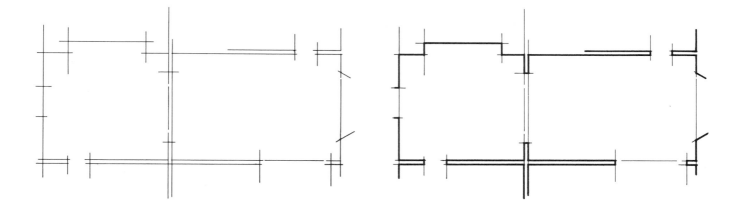

LINE WEIGHTS

The hard thing is knowing how heavy to make each line. Since what we are drawing here is referred to as a "base drawing" (one that will serve as the base for future, more elaborate renderings), it should be made of lines that are consistently dark, crisp, and accurately positioned. This will allow the lines to be read through easily when you later on lay a new sheet of paper over this one to trace the outlines. That will in turn mean that drawings you make over the base will be accurate. Errors tend to multiply as copies or tracings are made, so it is important to strive for initial accuracy and easy tracing. Line weights remain a most important subject once you know what to include in your drawing, so they will receive further attention in Chapter 4.

WHAT TO SHOW

Your room, house, or apartment is full of things, so the question of what to show in the measured survey inevitably comes up. The basic vocabulary of architecture is rather small, however, and consists of walls, openings in walls, floor and ceiling planes, and columns and beams. These are the pieces to show. We are building incrementally here, and for now we only need what is *structural* (meaning either built-in or essential to the continued integrity of the building). The beauty of taking our plan slice at windowsill height is that we are able to include a remarkable amount of three-dimensional information in this one drawing.

To best support the flow of information, plan detail has been somewhat conventionalized. The conventions include ways of showing windows, doors, and stairs. Study the drawing labels below. Each line shown corresponds to a line in reality, and its omission would make the drawing look less credible.

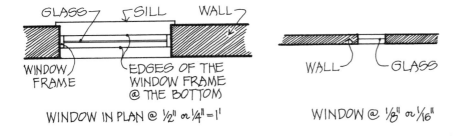

Doors are represented open at right angles to the wall they occur in. The quarter circle used to connect the open door to the wall vividly represents the piece of floor that needs to be kept clear so the door, when swinging, won't bang into anything.

STAIRS

The hardest thing to learn to show in plan is stairs. That is because they penetrate floor planes and therefore seem to be in conflict with much of our spatial thinking, which is based in the plan. A rather abstract convention exists for showing them.

Stairs depart from floors and in rising pass through the horizontal cut of plans. Of course, the stairs are cut too. In many buildings there is another stair below the one cut. It is the one that starts from the same floor as the one we are considering, but goes *down* to the floor below. These stairs are superimposed—they occupy the same position on plan, but are one story apart.

If you remember that in plans we show everything that is beneath the plane of the cut, you will realize that in showing stairs it is necessary to show the rising-up stair to the point where it passes through the cut plane, as well as the dropping-down stair that is revealed by removing the part above. It is easier to explain this in a drawing than in words.

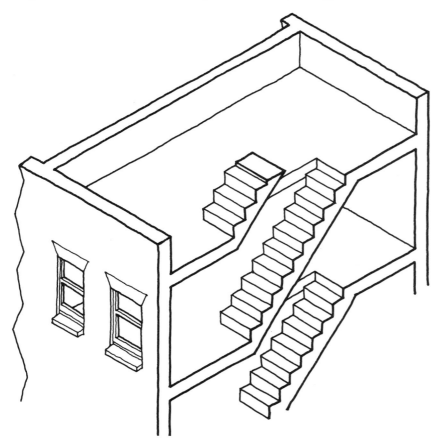

A literal plan view of the above gives us what appears to be an undifferentiated straight run:

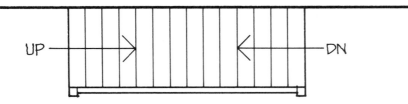

which is very confusing.

Architects have developed a convention that allows them to make clear the fact that two runs are being shown. They break—or cut—the rising-up stair with a diagonal line (to prevent that cut from being confused with the edges of the treads). This simple device, then, allows you to illustrate two superimposed stairs, one going up from the floor you are drawing and one going down.

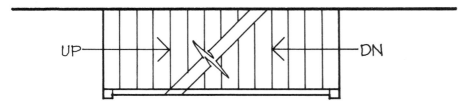

39

If you are showing only a single run of stairs (as, for instance, one coming up from a basement), then you need only show the stair rising to the height of the plan section and cut off by a diagonal. Of course, following our plan logic, you would also show whatever was beneath the portion of stair that you removed.

LAYING OUT STAIRS

Architects and designers have a trick for laying out stairs and other regularly divided pieces of a building. It is based on the fact that the space between two parallel lines can be divided into equal increments by measuring out regular divisions along any line between those parallel lines, including a diagonal one.

First draw two horizontal lines as far apart as the floors are in your design. Be sure to use the floor-to-floor height, not the floor-to-ceiling height. Now figure out how many risers will be needed to connect the two floors. A comfortable riser in residential work measures between 7″ and 8″ high. I find the number of risers by dividing the floor-to-floor height, expressed in inches, by 7.5 (the midpoint of the acceptable range) and then rounding the answer to the nearest whole number. For example, if you have a 9′ floor-to-floor height (108″) and you divide it by 7.5″, you will get 14.4 as the answer. Rounding down suggests that 14 risers is what you need. As a check, I divide 108″ by 14, which tells me that each riser will be 7.71″ high, a comfortable height.

Now lay a scale over the two horizontal floor lines. Use the same scale as you did for laying out the drawing. Place its 0 gradation on one line. Pivot the scale around this point until the gradation corresponding to the number of risers you need (14 for our example) is over the other line.

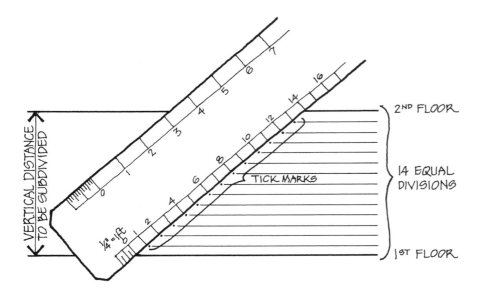

Make tick marks at each gradation. Remove the scale and draw faint lines with your 4H lead through each tick and parallel to the two floor lines. You should have equal increments.

Next, locate the starting point of your stair. It is usually a few feet from a door or some equivalent boundary. You will need one tread fewer than you did risers. In residential construction architects generally follow the stair proportions established by François Blondel in the 17th century. Reduced to a rule of thumb, they suggest that R + T = 17.5″, or Rise

+ Tread = 17.5″. If we work backward, 17.5″ − R = T will give you the tread width appropriate to your riser height. To determine the stairs' total length, multiply the tread width by the number of treads you need. Now measuring from the stairs' starting point, lay out the distance you've just calculated, and make a second vertical line at this point. Using the trick with the diagonal scale, subdivide the distance between the two lines. Make a series of faint lines through the second set of ticks. You will be left with a faint grid.

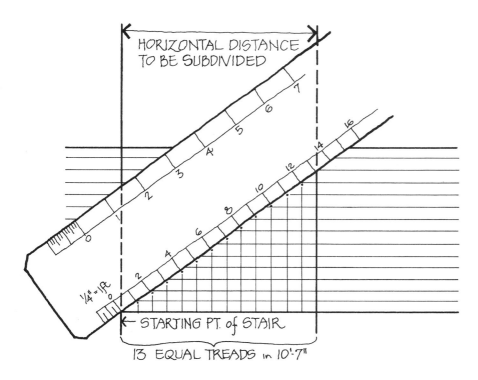

Now go back and heavy up the individual treads and risers as appropriate.

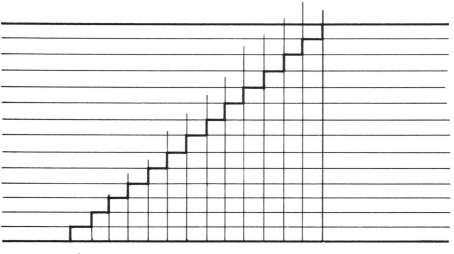

"HEAVIED-UP" STAIR PROFILE

LINES ABOVE AND LINES BELOW

At some point in your designing you will doubtless need to show on a plan something that exists above it—for instance, a skylight—or below it—perhaps an excavated crawl space under a floor. This information will be needed because what happens above or below can very strongly influence the quality of a space. Though the information may also show on sections or other floor plans, it is occasionally essential to show it combined with the space it has the most powerful impact on. Designers include such information in dashed-line form and usually note that what is shown is above or below.

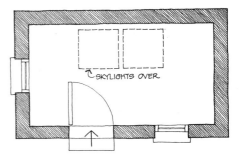

SECTION DRAWING

Vertical sections—usually simply called "sections"—are the drawings that turn your plan ideas into volumes. They are essential design drawings, and presentation of your design thinking is impossible without them.

Sections in a design presentation convey vertical information to augment horizontal information contained in a plan. They must be cut at meaningful points in the design; in other words, they must look into important parts of a design. One such point is at a staircase. Here the section allows us to understand the means for moving from floor to floor, the relationship of the downstairs volume to the upstairs one, and so forth.

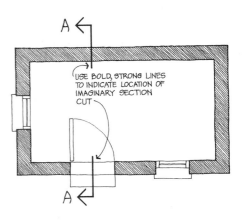

So that a viewer can understand at a glance where a section was cut or taken, there is a convention for showing that information on plan. What amounts to a bent arrow is placed on either side of the plan where the cut was made. The arrow can be allowed to overlap the outside walls of the building, but it never is run across the plan. An extra line there could be confused with some essential other line and would then impede understanding. Both arrowheads that make one section cut are labeled A or B or whatever. The section drawings themselves are labeled "Section A-A" or "Section B-B."

Section cuts are sometimes "cranked" or bent on their way through a space. This allows a single section to meander back and forth to reveal important information that a straight-line cut could not show. Where such a section turns inside the plan, a signal is given to the viewer in the form of two attached, right-angled lines—an L—that indicate the changed direction of the cut. Possibly because of this, such sections are popularly called "cranked."

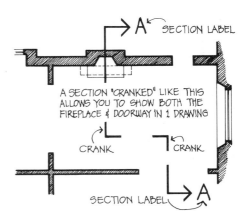

Design sections differ from construction sections in that they are not usually concerned with the materials of construction, but rather with informing us unambiguously of what is solid and what is void so that we can better understand the designed volumes. To do this they are frequently rendered in much the same way that plans are, and the walls, ceilings, and floors that are cut through are pochéd, or rendered dark. Even if you don't render these elements, remember to use the heaviest lines in your drawings for the pieces of the building that are cut to make the section. You should refer to Chapter 4 for a further discussion of rendering and line weights.

A section drawing that is part of your apartment or home survey exercise can be made in either of two ways: you may use dimensions off the same survey you used for the plan supplemented by height information, or you can first draw up the plan and then lay out the section over it, simply tracing the relevant horizontal dimensions as you need them. I prefer the latter method since I believe it to be both quicker and more accurate.

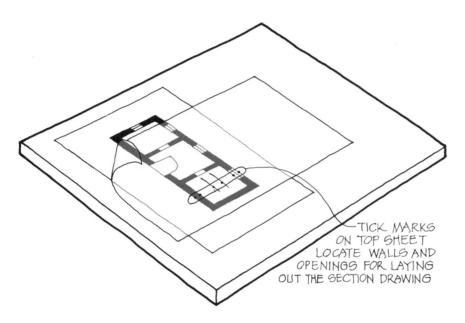

TICK MARKS ON TOP SHEET LOCATE WALLS AND OPENINGS FOR LAYING OUT THE SECTION DRAWING

How do you figure out how thick the floor is? Measure it at the stairwell.

THE ELEVATION

Elevations are frequently the only drawings in the initial triad in which materials are rendered. That is because their subjects—building facades—are typically fairly flat. The other two drawings are sections and are therefore concerned by definition with depth, with the illusion of three dimensions. By contrast, elevations typically reveal a two-dimensional composition, a play of sizes and materials. The rendering reveals those materials.

It is difficult to accurately render the materials of facades since most scales we use are too small to allow much detail. What you should strive for is the impression the materials leave in the mind's eye—a buildup of horizontal layers in the case of brick, strong horizontal banding of shadow in the case of clapboards, and so on.

More information on rendering conventions is contained in Chapter 4.

Elevations are labeled with the names of the compass directions they face. This is hard to understand and remember for many people who think of themselves standing in front of a facade looking the opposite way from that indicated on the drawing. For example, why doesn't the label read, "Elevation looking south"? The label really has to do with what direction the *house* is looking—with what exposure to light and weather that facade will receive. English architects label their drawings, "Elevation to the north" or "Elevation to the east," which seems a wise and unambiguous style.

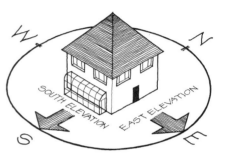

Elevations are usually drawn after the plan and section have been begun. If you set up your drawing board as shown below, you will find it easy to "generate" an elevation.

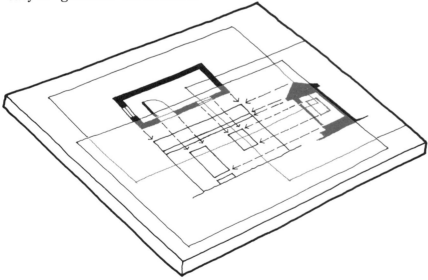

Remember if you are making elevations this way, trace through the outer edges of the exterior walls, not the inner, as you would if you were making a section.

Elevations may also be drawn of interior walls. Such drawings have much in common with sections, which frequently show inside wall planes, making interior elevations unnecessary. An interior elevation is useful, however, in explaining a wall that has a lot going on in it—as, for example, a hotel lobby wall might.

FURTHER DETAIL

Now that you have completed your three base drawings, you will want to add embellishments that will enhance the illusion of depth, give visual scale to your design—usually in the form of the human figure—provide information about construction materials (usually only on the facades), and reveal patterns of space use through placement of furnishings. Such embellishments are loosely joined under the name "rendering" and are the subject of the next chapter.

CHAPTER FOUR

LINES, TONE, AND RENDERING

This chapter is concerned both with *lines*—what line weights to use for various purposes—and with the embellishment of the line drawings we have discussed so far. That embellishment is usually called "rendering."

Design drawings are two-dimensional, planar representations of a three-dimensional universe. Anyone who draws for presentation wants therefore to conjure up for viewers as much "realism"—in the form of depth or plasticity and detail—as possible. The vocabulary available for this consists of only three things: lines, white space, and tone. Since the white space is there from the beginning and we act on it only to reduce it, our assertive repertoire actually consists of lines and tone.

LINES

Lines in nature occur very seldom. Though human constructs have made straight edges commonplace, there are few lines as lines in the natural world. Reality is made up of solid stuff—substance bounded by planes or surfaces.

In most of our drawing we represent planes by their borders—with *lines*. These borders reality defines by changes of texture or color or value (meaning brightness) or direction. In line drawing we use lines to hold edges and let the white cream cheese of the paper suggest both empty space and surface. It sometimes seems that we conspire to understand this deviation from reality, and the conspiracy, I suspect, is simply that we have been trained from birth to accept drawn lines as the boundaries of planes and objects that in nature have color and texture to map their existence to our eyes—and few, if any, lines!

It is important to recognize before we proceed that line drawing is a sophisticated abstraction from reality, a conventional shorthand tacitly agreed to by architects and designers. It is by no means the only way to represent our designs, as a visit to any museum of art will reveal. Most of the paintings produced in the history of the world have been concerned with reproducing surface and value. A drawing style for architects and designers that more accurately reflected value and surface—say, a "painterly" style—would be more realistic, but would also be more time-consuming to produce. The compromise we arrive at, therefore, is to make line drawings and to add tone and surface detail to those used to communicate the "feel" of our designs—our presentation drawings.

Qualities of Lines. Line has two principal characteristics: direction and weight. Direction—determined by you—makes a line an arrow, or ray traveling through space, that evokes that space and makes objects of it.

Line weight refers to the width of the line on paper. Width means blackness, and blackness attracts the eye.

There are conventions about line weights that need to be balanced against what you are trying to do in the drawing as a whole. In general, use a heavy (dark) line for the edge (of the plane) that is nearest to the viewer and progressively lighter lines for parts of the drawing that are farther away. There are exceptions caused by differences of intent—realism versus emphasis—that will be discussed in greater detail later in this chapter. For now let's look at a standard.

The sequence or ranking of line weights generally observed (going from thickest to thinnest) is:

1. *Profile lines,* or lines that separate foreground from undifferentiated background, should be heaviest. Use these lines for the edges of walls that are cut in making a section, though not in the one case described in 2 below.

2. *Section edges* receive slightly less emphasis than profile lines in an oblique view such as an axonometric or perspective drawing.

3. *Edges of major distinct components* of your design that may be in nearly the same plane as other components, but that are separated from them, are shown with the next thickest line. These are a sort of "inside" profile line.

4. *Lines within planes and objects* in the space, such as furniture or window sash lines in an elevation, have the next thinner lines.

5. *Texture lines* and rendering within one plane get the next thinner line.

6. *Dimensioning and assembly lines* should be the lightest you intend to have read in a final drawing or print.

7. *Construction lines,* also sometimes called "layout lines," should virtually disappear after you have heavied up the drawing.

All the above are illustrated on page 48.

It is often difficult to figure out *how* to make this many different lines. After all, if you put pencil to paper, it makes a mark. Of course, as we discussed in Chapter 2, a softer lead will lay down more graphite under a similar pressure than a harder one will, but it also wears away quicker to a wider mark and is hard to control. In the end drafters use several techniques to achieve line difference. One is to use various hardnesses of lead. Two is to use different pressures, with all the attendant problems. Three is to make several parallel lines side by side for heavy lines. This last technique allows the use of a hard lead while still permitting the creation of heavy lines. I recommend it to my students.

With ink drawing the problem is simpler, since the technical pens we use are each designed to make a separate and distinct line width. However, experience and judgment are needed to select appropriate line weights (point diameters) for any particular drawing. The bulk of the illustrations in this book have been drawn with a no. 3 technical pen point (.8 mm) and a no. 0 (.35 mm) point. Where I have needed a finer line, I have used a 00 (.30 mm) or a 4 × 0 (.18 mm). These are the same nibs I use in making most presentations at ¼″ = 1′ scale.

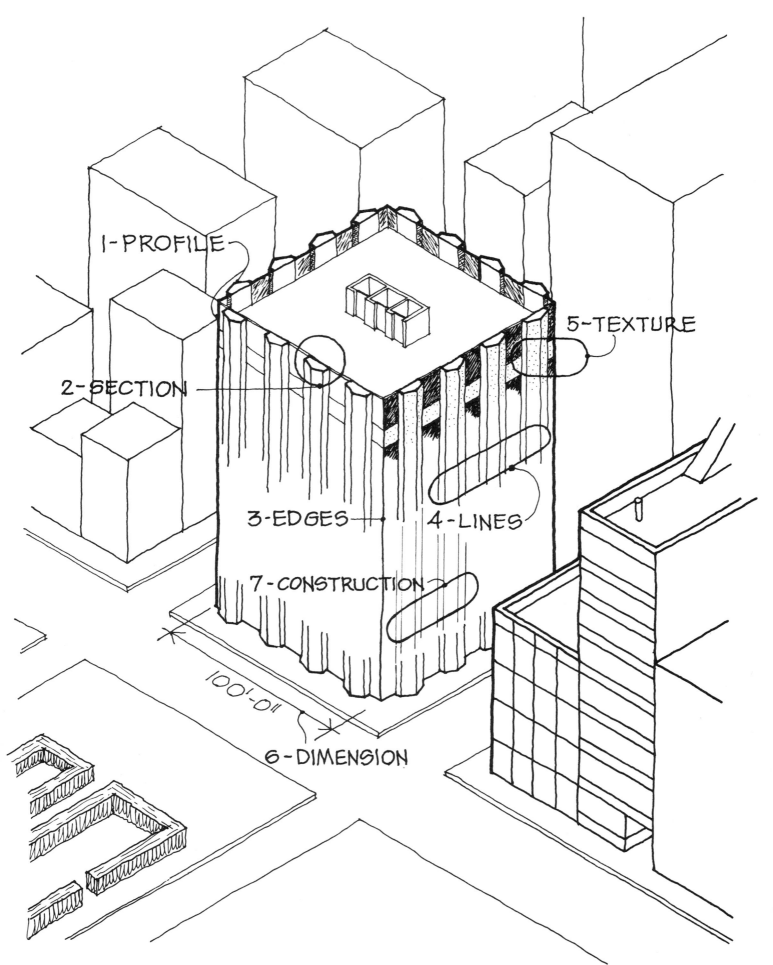

1-PROFILE

2-SECTION

3-EDGES

4-LINES

5-TEXTURE

6-DIMENSION

7-CONSTRUCTION

100'-0"

TONE

Tone is applied to the line drawings architects and designers make to "hold" surfaces—that is, to differentiate planes from others around them more surely than lines at the edges or corners can do. Tones have other uses, which we will discuss, but in a world of line drawings, they principally hold surfaces and create planar differences and contrasts.

Practically, tones are used both for rendering walls that are cut through in a plan or a vertical section—called "pochéing" and further described below—or for simulating the play of light—in the form of shade and shadow. A full investigation of tone would involve the study of both freehand drawing and the laws of physics that govern light. Such an investigation is beyond the scope of this book, although we can certainly begin it here.

The tones we use are frequently made up of "particles" of black mixed with the white of the paper, as opposed to uniform areas of gray. These are the tones we make ourselves in the form of dots (also called "stipple"), methodical scribble, or crosshatching, using the same media we use for lines. Most design drawings are prepared this way because they must be reproduced, and the cheapest reproductions are high-contrast diazo prints—that is, black- or blue-line prints. Producing tones with the same medium you used to create lines throughout a drawing ensures that all marks in it will be of related densities and contrasts and will therefore with all probability all be reproducible.

To produce tones with a pencil the following techniques, among others, are useful:

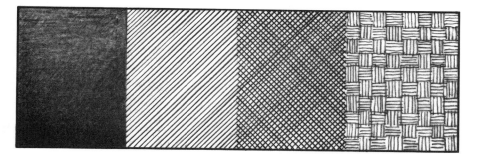

To produce tones with pen and ink the following techniques, also among others, are useful:

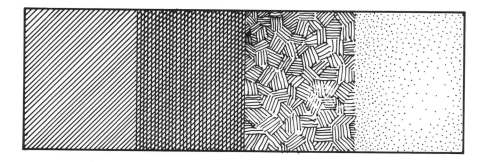

Tones can also be made by different media than you used for the lines, by transfer films, or even by the addition of a layer of tracing paper on top of your base sheet.

Of course, color is a form of tone, but its use is beyond the scope of this book. Refer to the Selected Bibliography for an excellent book on the use of color.

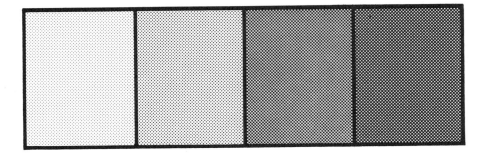

Line + Tone = Rendering. Both lines and tones are used by architects and designers to "render" their drawings. Rendering is the treatment of a drawing to enhance its ability to communicate spatial information and surface texture. One of the major purposes of rendering is to create the illusion of depth that enhances the viewers' understanding of space and volume. This is done by "layering" surfaces so our eyes perceive them to be one on top of another. A second purpose is to help the viewer know what materials the drawn object is to be constructed of. A third is to reveal the play of light on the forms of the design.

It is both possible and usually desirable to combine these purposes. First you must determine what you want to achieve with your rendering.

PURPOSES OF RENDERING

In presentation drawing it is always contrast or blackness that gets the attention. The darkest area of the drawing pulls the eye to it and dominates the rest. If you want to emphasize something, render it dark. This can also work against you: too much emphasis leaves you with a drawing that looks crude and heavy-handed. In rendering possibly the most important thing to keep in mind is that you must not overrender and defeat your purpose. It is important, therefore, to get into the habit of testing your previsualized rendering technique well before you are engaged in the last-minute rush, or "charrette." We will say more about this later.

In general, I try to render my drawings so that I need a minimum of lettering to explain them. This means that I use rendering to provide visual clues about the space, just as I use it to provide information hatching to show either 1″ or 2″ size tile and also to denote that the space is a bath- or powder room. These sizes of tile are most often used in bathrooms, and virtually everyone alive today who is likely to read these pages will automatically associate that tight tile pattern with bathroom floors. I therefore don't need to label the room. In kitchens, where reinforced vinyl tile is common, I usually draw a 9″ or 12″ square grid of lines on the floor for the same reasons of denotation, since these are the two common sizes of these tiles. In fact, in my residential work I use seamless vinyl for kitchen floors. The point is that in my drawings I use visual devices, generally understood, to help explain what is going on in a space.

Some Definitions Before We Proceed. . . . We need to clarify our terminology here. Architects and designers have used perspective drawings to communicate with clients since the dawn of time. These perspectives are frequently rendered, for the reasons previously discussed. In recent decades such perspectives have often been produced by specialists, who have come to be called "renderers." The perspective drawings they produce have come to be called "renderings." In this book we will use the term "rendering" solely in the sense of embellishment to drawings, since that embellishment can, in fact, be applied equally to plan, section, elevation, and all the oblique views. Perspective drawings we will call "perspective drawings" or just "perspectives."

Light, Distance, and Rendering. There are two approaches to the use of lines and tones that architects and other designers generally try to follow. Those approaches are based on the modern world's knowledge of the psychological value of line and on the Renaissance world's knowledge of optics and visual perception.

Modern artists and illustrators—including cartoonists—have learned from physiologists and psychologists that seeing takes place largely in the brain (as opposed to the eye) and that what the brain perceives may differ from what the eye is shown. This elaborated knowledge requires that the outline of any particular object or detail be darkest and inside lines lightest. Our gestalt for closed, completed forms is satisfied by this hierarchy.

The painterly or Renaissance tradition requires that objects nearest the viewer be shown darkest and those farthest away be lightest. An understanding of aerial (or atmospheric) perspective explains this. Light rays are scattered in the atmosphere by particles of dust and by drops of water vapor. Those light rays reaching the eye from farther objects are weaker (and the image they produce is lighter) than those traveling from closer by, because they have been subjected to greater dispersion. Any object so observed also appears paler in color (less saturated) than its counterpart nearer the observer.

For a drawing to work for architects it must satisfy both the modern and the Renaissance ideas.

RENDERING A VARIETY OF OBJECTS AND FORMS

In rendering, as in choice of line weight, there are conventions that assist understanding. Think of what follows as minimum techniques.

Walls. The first rendering usually applied to any plan or section drawing is a darkening of the walls cut through to that particular section. This is called "pochéing," a word held over from the French Beaux-Arts method of teaching design. By rendering the cut walls dark, you denote that what is there is perceived as solid and heavy; it is what you have carved up to create the volumes of your design. It also indicates what can be walked through and what can't, and it signals the viewer that the wall represented in fact rises up from the plane of the floor and continues past the plane of the section. The pochéing also visually bounds the floor plane and produces a contrast between wall and floor that can be read by a viewer standing several feet away.

For most of my presentation drawings I use a freehand ink tracing, made with rather bold, heavy lines, and a marker—something like an Ad Warm Gray no. 7—to poché the walls. Outlines of the walls (profile lines) I make with a no. 3 Mars pen, and inside rendering of texture I do with progressively lighter pen points or with pencil. The number of the marker I use or the number of pen depends on what other tones I have decided to use in the drawing.

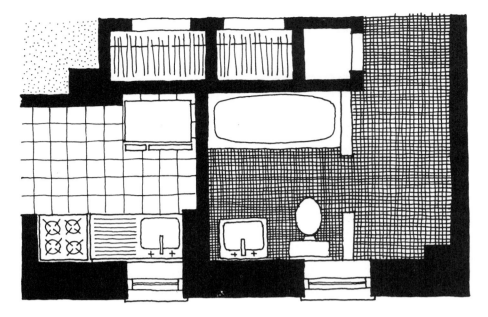

Of course, there are other ways of pochéing. The most traditional is crosshatching, both drafted and freehand.

You may also want to poché your walls in solid black or use a pencil tone.

Materials. The most frequently rendered materials are wood, stone (such as marble), brick, concrete, and glass. Wood in furniture and in large, vertically mounted panels is shown thus with a generalized wood graining.

Where wood is used in narrow boards (such as clapboards), its grain is not shown, but the effect of the boarding is created by its shadow lines:

Vertical wood siding, such as board-and-batten or tongue-and-groove (also sometimes called "v-groove") or Texture 1-11 plywood, is also shown principally by shadow lines:

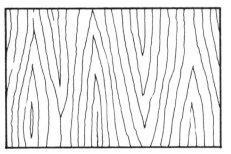

Generalized wood grain.

Wood clapboards.

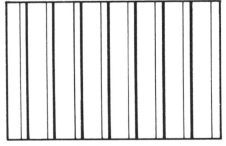

Vertical wood siding.

Polished stones like marble are shown by their veining, and you need to be careful not to make that too much like wood grain:

Rough-cut stone is sometimes rendered in tone, especially if its edges are square. For that kind of rendering it is useful to sharpen a fairly soft lead (say, an HB) to a chisel point so that you can make the broken planes in single strokes. In cases involving many random stones it is usually enough to show them with lines indicating their edges:

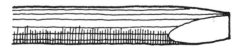

TRUE CHISEL POINT

Marble indicated by veining.

Fieldstone rendered in pencil.

Fieldstone indicated by its edges.

Brick as a rule is shown on drawings by a closely spaced horizontal banding. Since a standard brick is about 2″ high and only 8″ long, it is not possible to show individual bricks in most drawings.

Since concrete blocks are usually substantially larger than bricks, they are easier to render. It is usual to show them simply by their edges, with lines spaced appropriately. If the scale of your drawing is large you may want to include shadow lines at each joint. You should look in *Architectural Graphic Standards* (listed in the Selected Bibliography), to find the dimensions of standard building materials.

There doesn't seem to be general agreement on how to render concrete in architects' drawings. Some do it with a "wash" of tone, darkening that where the concrete is in shade, and others do it with a stripple of dots. You should experiment. Don't decide to do four full elevations in stipple and discover at the last moment that it will take you two full days to complete your drawings—and you have only two hours until you must present!

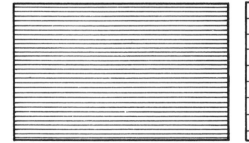
Brickwork.

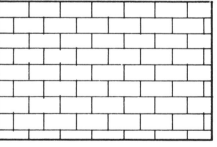
Concrete block or jumbo brick.

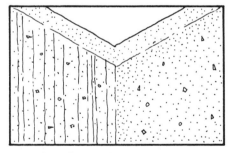
Board- and smooth-formed concrete.

Glass. Glass is a lively medium and one of the principal materials of 20th-century architecture. Its rendering, however, is frequently misunderstood, so a few notes about how it really works, coupled with field observation on your part, will help you understand its presentation.

Many people show windows in an elevation as the lightest elements in the drawing. In fact, if you are drawing an interior view looking out, the glass will look lighter than anything else in the view. But if you are drawing an exterior elevation or perspective, the windows will be dark. Buildings are like sponges or labyrinths: where there is a window, light falls through the facade into the interior, where most of it is trapped. Therefore, even if the building you are designing is made of some dark material, its walls will reflect more of the light that falls on them than its windows will. Obviously, there are exceptions. If the angle of view is precisely right, you will get a reflection of the sun, and the window will be very bright indeed. Also, of course, window glass is at least a little wavery, so you will get some reflection. But the fact is—and you should look out a window at another building right now to prove it to yourself—windows in a building seen in daylight are mostly dark.

Not all dark, however. Where there is glass there are reflections, and you must show them to make your rendering believable. Windows up high will reflect the clouds and sky, those down low people, the landscape, and the horizon. Reflections are best rendered paler and less distinctly than the rest of the drawing. After all, glass is *always* a most imperfect reflector unless coated to make a mirror and will let a lot of the light that falls on it leak away to the interior. Reflections in it are therefore always ephemeral and indistinct.

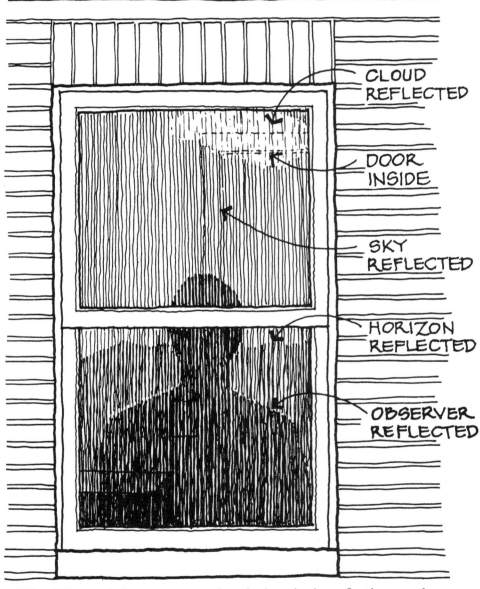

CLOUD
REFLECTED

DOOR
INSIDE

SKY
REFLECTED

HORIZON
REFLECTED

OBSERVER
REFLECTED

What I like to do in my presentations is draw in the reflections on the back of the final piece of tracing paper. Then, working on the front, I take something like a warm gray no. 4 and make a few, quick streaks along the window glass area. Working very quickly, I then go over the whole area of the glass with a warm gray no. 1 to soften and spread the marks made with the no. 4. I am able to do this on final presentation drawings only; I have not found it possible to have this mixed-media technique printed very consistently. It also only works on some kinds of paper.

Entourage. "Entourage" is another word inherited from the École des Beaux-Arts. It means "surroundings," which include the surface of the earth, trees, shrubs, and other plants, paving, bodies of water, automobiles, furniture, and—most important of all—the human figure. There is no general agreement on how to show these items, so an exhaustive exploration of ways they are handled would require at least another volume. For our purposes some general observations and a few examples will suffice. You should, however, extend your range of choice by looking analytically at drawings you admire. Figure out how other renderers construct trees, figures, and so forth. Copy them. Imitation is a legitimate way of expanding your vocabulary. As you extend your knowledge and skills your own style will creep in and overwhelm the imitated one.

The Skin of the Earth. In a site plan, or any drawing that includes terrain, it is imperative that the surface of the earth be held by some sort of tone. If it is not, your building will seem to be afloat in a sea of cream cheese. Some ways to hold the surface include:

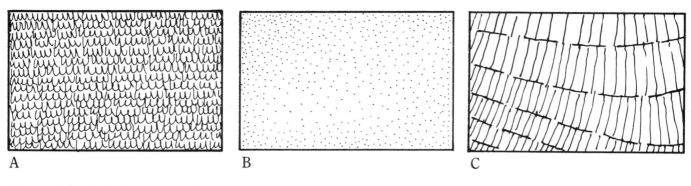

A   B   C

A is good for indicating grassy lawns; B suggests sand, gravel, or textured surfaces such as concrete; and C is especially useful where you have a lot of terrain to show and you want to emphasize its slope. The dashed lines here are height contour lines.

Trees. Trees in plan are relatively easy to draw. They are represented by their leaf crowns, which are generalized to a circular shape that can be started either with a circle template or a compass.

Once you establish the positions and sizes of the trees with light circles, go back and heavy up the profile of the tree mass. Sometimes two lines are better than one.

FREQUENTLY BETTER IN PENCIL ⌐

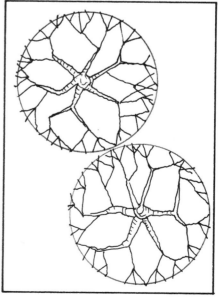

This kind of drawn tree is most useful to architects because any piece of a design that is overlapped by the tree's leaf crown can still be shown. The leaf crown is treated as though it were transparent. The profile is shown with a heavy line, and whatever happens underneath is also shown, though with a lighter line than adjacent areas that are not filtered through an intervening medium (shown at the top of the next page).

Where the tree is freestanding (and appears in a drawing of fairly large scale), it is typical to show a branch pattern as shown on the right.

Transfer trees, like transfer letters, are made by several companies. They consist of tree forms printed on plastic backup sheets. A releasing agent between the ink and the backup allows the ink to be transferred onto another surface (such as drafting vellum) when the backup sheet is rubbed systematically.

Transfer trees are too heavy to please my eye. If I'm going to use mechanical aids to make trees, I will use a tree stamp, either purchased at the right scale or carved to size from an artgum eraser.

Trees in elevation are a very long story. For a start, there are a great many varieties. Each has a characteristic proportional relationship between height and width. Each has a characteristic branching pattern and relationship of stem mass to leaf crown.

When you draw them try to remember the following general points:

1. Where a new branch takes off from the main stem in deciduous trees, that main stem will change direction slightly to counterbalance the weight of the new branch. If you draw tree trunks with a chisel-pointed lead, you should stop your line where you want to add a branch.

2. The total cross-sectional area of a tree trunk at its base is approximately the same as the cross-sectional area of its main branches. What this means is that if you draw in too many branches, the tree will look top-heavy and unrealistic.

3. The sphere of soil occupied by a tree's roots is approximately the same size as the sphere of air occupied by its leaf crown. Recognizing this fact can help you draw believable trees near buildings or in tubs.

Leaves are needed to turn your stems into trees. Leaves may be generalized or particularized. The particularized leaves can take a very long time to draw.

The amount of detail required is directly related to the scale of the drawing and to the nearness or farness of the tree to the plane of the drawing. Again, look at trees drawn by renderers you admire. Imitate them.

Water. Water in rendering seems to be best shown by a series of squiggly lines representing a wind ripple. Though I have never had to draw a dead-calm reflecting pool, I imagine it would be shown in much the same way that reflections in windows are. The squiggly lines look best if they are drawn parallel to the horizon, no matter what the orientation of the pool edges or lake or ocean bulkhead or beach may be.

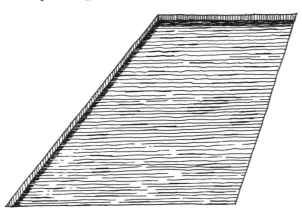

Reflections in the water are made either with a heavier squiggly line or by adding extra lines. Remember that the reflection should start where what is reflected meets the ground, so if there is some land between the bottom of the building and the beginning of the water, only part of the building will be reflected in the water. The rest of its "reflection" falls on a nonreflecting surface—the earth.

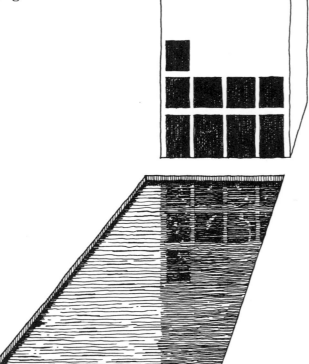

58

The Human Figure. The human figure is the most important single embellishment you can add to a drawing. Its size varies in adults surprisingly little, so the placement of a human figure in a drawing informs viewers about the sizes of other things represented there. Although you could achieve the same result with written dimensions and dimension lines, you would clutter up your drawings with reading matter and still not create the sense of size relationships engendered by the human figure.

Of course, the use of human figures also adds life to your designs and emphasizes space and volume as containers of human activities. No design presentation should be without figures.

Average heights of men and women in the United States today are approximately 5'10" and 5'4½", respectively. To make a human figure in realistic proportions at large scale, I start by measuring off one of these heights and then subdividing it into 7 to 7½ parts.

Topmost of these is the head. The width of the body is approximately equal to 2 of these parts (that is, 2 heads laid sideways equal the maximum width of the body). The shoulders begin approximately 1⅓ heads down and are slighly less than 2 heads wide. It is the elbow-belly region that reaches the maximum width. The crotch is about 3 heads above the floor, and the shoulders about 3 heads above that:

The foregoing gives you the approximate proportions of the human figure. Now we need to decide *how* to show it in our drawings.

I find that a fully rendered human figure looks awkward in architectural drawings. It seems to be in competition with the building around it. What I like to do is show the figure in outline only. This serves to add both the scale and vitality of the human figure to my drawings, while allowing the viewer to focus on the architecture.

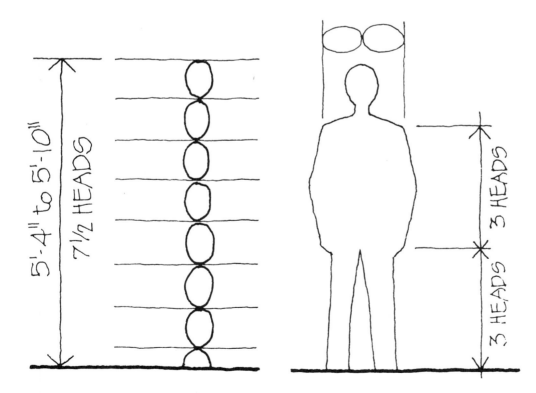

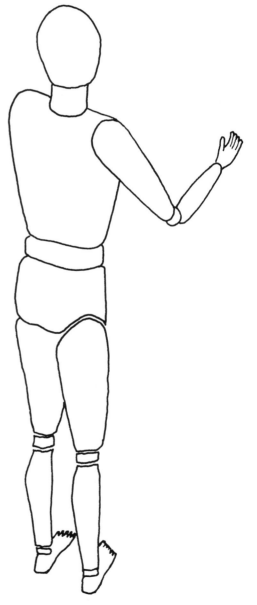

At a smaller scale the figure can be shown with a couple of hairpins and a blob.

It is hard to develop the ability to draw the human figure easily and correctly. It takes a good deal of practice. The effort is well directed, however, since the figure adds so much to your drawings. If you can afford it, you may find owning an artist's movable-joint figure like the one shown useful.

These are now moulded in plastic and are relatively inexpensive. Another, cheaper source of examples is magazine photographs, which you can keep in a file. When you have a large enough collection you will be able to find a figure for any drawing need.

Furniture. After the human figure, the most important single embellishment you can make to a plan is to furnish it. Recognizable chairs, tables, sofas, beds, and bureaus on a plan trigger mental processes that allow viewers to "feel" our designs. Stark white plans with no embellishment are scaleless and hard to read. The addition of furniture is both essential and fairly easy. The key here is to realize that you are striving for an impression of the occupied space—not a recreation of the world. The impression can be created with a few, rather generalized, "architectural" pieces of furniture—no Chippendale needed.

Students of architecture are often astonished to discover that the sizes of furniture fall within narrow and clearly defined limits. They shouldn't be—their bodies know the truth. The height of a chair seat above the ground is pretty tightly related to the length of the lower leg, and that only varies (in 90 percent of the adults of the human species) by a very few inches. Yes, there are differences between desk chairs and living room chairs, but the differences all work downward from the height established by the most erect posture (that is, most nearly the true length of the lower leg, in this case). Beds have the same height limitations. Table and desk heights are related to the height of the elbow above the ground when the elbow is attached to a seated person.

Since we are striving for an impression of the inhabited space, architects and designers have developed a generalized style of furniture that looks as though it were put together from sugar cubes. This is because it is squared up to be constructable with t-squares and triangles. The 20th century appears to have adopted this generalized style and has provided

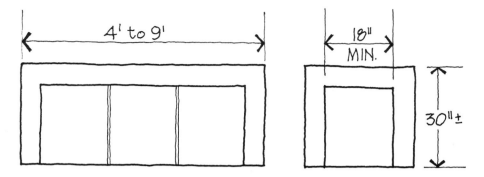

us with furniture entirely composed of right angles. Some of it even works for its users.

Dining tables are not standardized, though again human dimensions control the low end of the range. A table should be 36″ across to accommodate two face-to-face dinner plates and whatever serving paraphernalia is placed between them. The linear width unit should be at least 18″ for the same reason it is for chairs, though 24″ will make for more pleasant dining. Clearance between a table edge and a nearby wall should be enough to allow passage behind the seated diner of someone with a serving bowl—or a minimum of 2′6″.

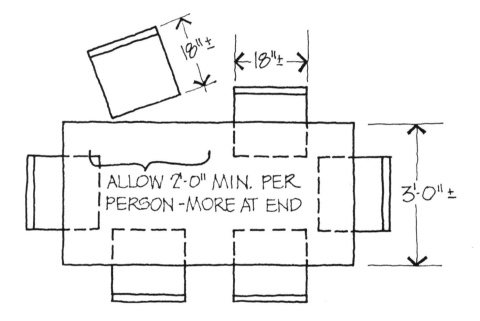

Not surprisingly, manufacturers of sheets and mattresses have come to agreement on a few standard sizes, which simplifies the stocking of sheets by retail outlets. The standard sizes are:

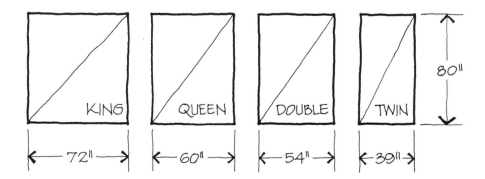

Closet depths are related to the width of the human frame, in this case hung from a hangar. The standard minimum clear inside depth (front to back) is 22″. Modern designers usually allow a total of 2′0″ from the back of a closet to the front of its doors, though these will be of the thin, lightweight, "bifold" variety. The 22″ clear is enough to allow clothing to be hung up without rubbing against a wall and to have room to "breathe."

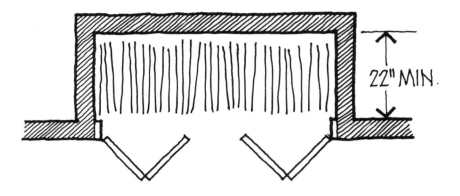

Kitchens are also subject to standards, though these have as much to do with manufacturing exigencies as with the human frame. The usual depth of a kitchen counter is 25″, though the effective depth in a modern kitchen is usually substantially less than that because of all the small appliances, decorative tiles, baskets, canisters, and so on that people insist on collecting. There are standard increments of height: the most usual 36″ for the top of the counter above the floor and another 18″ for the height of the lowest shelf in the wall-hung cabinets above, though this is true only where the upper cabinets are not also over a stove or some other appliance. Where they are, clearance dimensions are usually regulated by building codes.

There isn't room here to go into all the sizes of all the objects we are familiar with. There also isn't reason to; other books have covered the subject thoroughly. Some of them are listed in the Selected Bibliography. However, we have looked at enough sizes for you to be able to construct believable furniture.

Shade and Shadow. One of the most necessary rendering skills to acquire is knowledge of casting shadows, for it will allow you to study the play of light in and on your designs and to add striking depth and realism to your drawings. Conventions that are fairly easy to learn and use exist for shadows and grow out of the tools of the profession. It is important for you to realize that what these conventions allow is not a real study of the play of light, but is a generalization. You should pursue the subject of light and buildings further than we can take it in this book. We will explore only the shadow-casting conventions here. An excellent book concerned with the study of light is listed in the Selected Bibliography.

We need to establish some definitions before we proceed. The dictionary makes virtually no distinction between the words "shade" and "shadow," although architects and artists make a distinct difference to help distinguish two visual phenomena.

On the side of a building turned away from the light there is, quite naturally, an absence of direct light. This part of the object is said to be in *shade*. Extending from that shaded side in the opposite direction from the light source is a trace—or outline—of the object that is called its *shadow*.

The shadow almost always falls on another, adjacent surface, but may in some circumstances fall on a portion of the object that causes the shadow. Note a fundamental difference: shade is dark because light can't reach it, shadow because an object prevents light from reaching a surface that would otherwise be directly illuminated.

For all practical purposes such differences are not significant. However, since they are well established, we will observe them here. Remember: shade is what we observe on the side of an object turned away from the light. Shadow is the trace that object makes on another surface by blocking the light that would otherwise fall there.

For years I believed, as I had been taught, that shade is lighter than shadow. This is not necessarily true. It is true that we sometimes perceive that shadow is darker than shade. I believe this is because the eye usually finds shadows on the ground and casts a raking glance along them. That produces an apparent "compaction" of the surface in shadow, which emphasizes its darkness. Surfaces in shade, on the other hand, are usually parallel to the observer and are therefore not subject to this compaction. The phenomenon that causes real differences to occur between surfaces that are in either shade or shadow is the "borrowing" of light that is dispersed in the atmosphere either by dust and water vapor or by reflections. Such light can cause substantial differences of illumination. In the city vertical faces of buildings seem to receive more borrowed light (because of reflections) than the ground does, and as they are the ones that are usually in shade, it seems that shade is lighter than shadow.

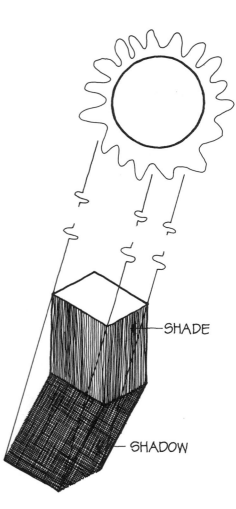

— SHADE

— SHADOW

Some Rules about Shadows. In thinking about shadows you should remember the following:

1. Light rays are regarded as being parallel to each other. The sun is 93 million miles away, and we on earth therefore subtend a tiny segment of the arc into which the sun radiates. Each of the rays that reaches us may safely be assumed to be parallel to each other ray.

2. The shadow of a straight line will be a straight line so long as that shadow falls on a flat surface. In fact, if you could position yourself so that you could observe shadows from a position along the sun's rays, every shadow of a straight line would look straight, even where it fell on an uneven surface. The classic illustration of a shadow falling on a stair illustrates that point.

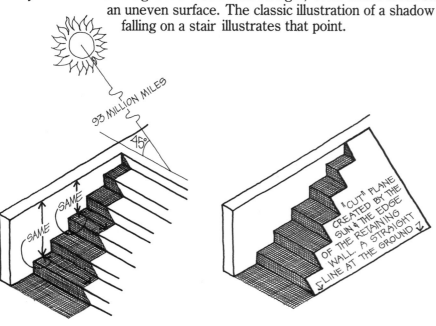

3. The shadow of an edge falling on a plane parallel to that edge will be exactly parallel to that edge and offset from it by a distance equal to the height of the object above the surface receiving the shadow (assuming that the light is falling in accordance with the convention described in the section on Shadow Casting below). I like to think of a circular cafe table here, hovering 27″ to 28″ above the ground on its pedestal base.

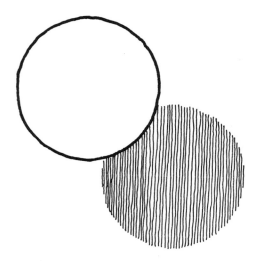

4. The shadow of a surface falling on a plane parallel to that surface will be exactly the same shape as the surface. In other words, the shadow of a flat-roofed building will be exactly the same shape as the roof, with the addition of lines that represent the shadows of the corners that hold up the roof.

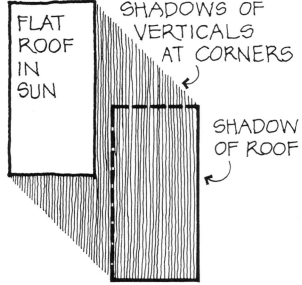

Shadow Casting. To understand the shadow-casting convention, you need to visualize a gigantic, transparent cube. In one (lower) corner is your building. Diagonally across the cube (in an upper corner) is the sun.

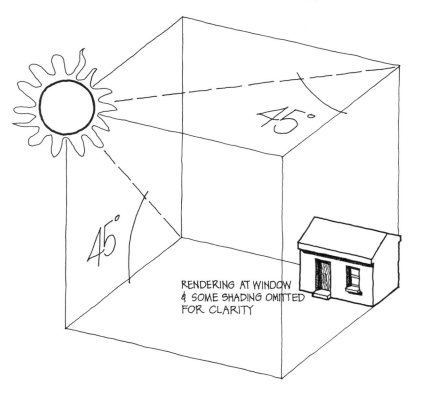

64

This is considered to be true for every facade of the building except the north, which usually does not have shadows cast on it. Now obviously if you are presenting several elevations together, you will want to make a consistent plan of how the shadows should be drawn. It is confusing to show drawings that suggest both morning sun (that is, from the east) and afternoon (from the west).

Since the shadows are seen in true elevation like the facades themselves, they will look as though the sun was above the building and to the right or left in such a position that its rays fall downward across the building at an angle of 45°.

Since the sun is also considered to be in front of and above the building, its rays penetrate or point into the facade at a plan angle of 45°.

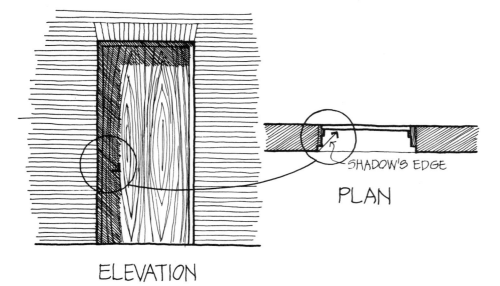

PLAN

ELEVATION

What all this means is that shadows cast according to this convention fall precisely as far from the edge casting them as that edge is distant (above, usually) from the surface receiving them. In turn, that means no computation for the renderer. You need simply scale off the distances from a section or plan and scale their equivalents into your rendering. You will find that working with a 45°-45°-90° triangle makes casting shadows at corners easy. The edges projected there are precisely as long as the length of the projection or incursion.

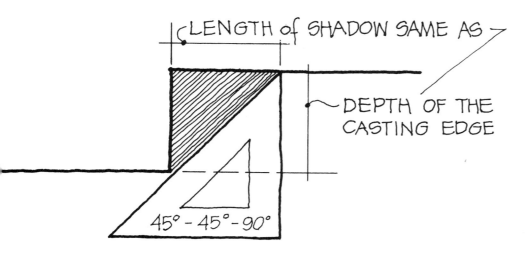

Where the building or object casting the shadow is positioned such that its shadows fall on a lower building or some other surface irregularity, you will have to do some figuring. It is simply the subtraction of the height of the incurring building from the height of the casting building.

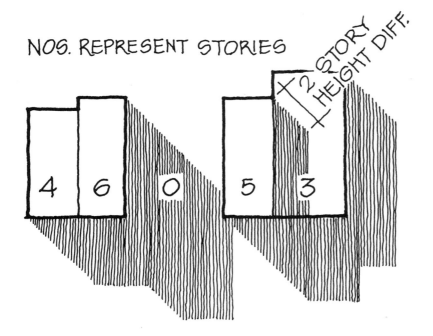

PUTTING IT ALL TOGETHER . . .

Always remember that your principal endeavor is designing and describing spaces. Rendering is intended to support that designing—and to supply some information about materials. Keep in mind the hierarchy of line weights, and make sure that the lines you use to describe what goes on within a surface—like woodgrain or floor tile lines—do not conflict in weight and importance with edges of planes and objects. In fact, take a moment now to really look at a tiled or boarded floor. Notice how inconsequential the lines between the tiles or the edges of the boards are in the total sense you have of the space you are in and of the plane they are in. Remember this when you render your plans, and don't allow what you show on the floor to dominate your drawing.

Rendering of materials and furniture is intended, as we indicated earlier, to support the designing and communicating of space. It is important to keep the amount of rendering in balance with the presentation of the space-limiting elements (usually walls). Overrendering can hurt a presentation, so it is important that you explore what you have in your mind's eye before you set to work on the final presentation drawings.

I advise my students to take a scrap of the same paper they will be presenting on and to trace a portion of one of their design drawings, including all detail they plan to include and using the pen points and markers they plan for the final. A test piece that is about 6″ × 12″ is usually sufficient. Once the study is finished, I suggest that they pin it up on a wall, stand 6′ to 10′ away, and examine how it looks. We draw with our eyes about 12″ from the paper, we view from a distance of several feet, and the difference is immense. If the test fails to satisfy you there is usually small loss of time involved, and directions for a further test are indicated by the results.

DESIGN THE PRESENTATION

Final presentations need to be designed just as projects do. It is therefore always a good idea to spend some time planning for and designing your presentation. In school especially it is easy to fall behind and to omit some essential drawing, or to present drawings of vastly unequal levels of completion. By designing the presentation, you can help yourself avoid these traps.

First think through all the drawings you will need to adequately explain your design. List them in writing. Now decide which drawing will be largest, and use that size to determine the sheet size for the whole set. Allow enough white space around your drawings—crowded sheets are hard to read and don't do justice to their contents.

Determine what orientation of the sheet (assuming it is not a square) will best suit all the drawings. Should the rectangle of the paper be vertically or horizontally positioned when it is hung on the wall? Horizontal formats are the most common, but are certainly not standard. Your decision here may lead you to rethink the size you decided on above. *All of the sheets should be oriented the same way.*

Next you must decide where to place the title block. Title blocks are standardized forms that contain all the information you must put on a drawing to ensure its proper identification. This includes your name. The worst sin you can commit against yourself here, I believe, is to omit your name from your drawings. Students do it over and over again. It places the people who review their work at an irritating disadvantage, which makes them cranky. Give them your name!

You must also inform your viewers of the scale (that is, ¼″ = 1′, or what have you) and of the location of north in relation to your plans, with a north arrow like one of these:

Of the name of the drawing (such as "elevation to the north" or "elevations"), of the title of the project presented, and the date.

The inclusion of a design instructor's name in a title block always leaves me wondering whether the student who does so has an egomaniac for an instructor or is trying to flatter someone so that he or she will overlook sloppy work. If you are in the former situation, then by all means include the name; if you are in the latter, then you should consider another field of study in which you can do good work and not need to flatter.

Decide where on your sheet you want to place the essential words. As a general rule the title of the project should be largest, the title of the drawing and your name smaller, and the scale and date smallest. The words should all be arranged in the title block, which mearly suggests grouping—they don't have to be in a block. You should look at some published drawings for ideas on how to design a title block. A typical one is shown on the next page.

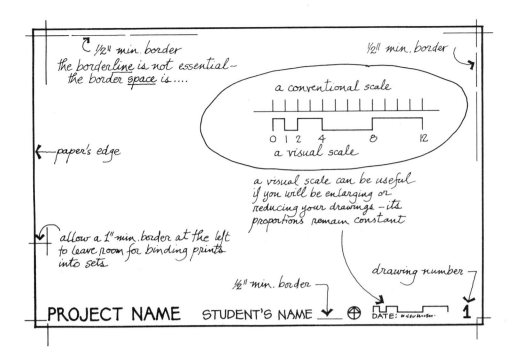

½" min. border
the borderline is not essential—
the border _space_ is....

½" min. border

a conventional scale

a visual scale

0 1 2 4 8 12

paper's edge

a visual scale can be useful
if you will be enlarging or
reducing your drawings — its
proportions remain constant

allow a 1" min. border at the left
to leave room for binding prints
into sets

½" min. border

drawing number

PROJECT NAME STUDENT'S NAME DATE: 1

For the type in my title blocks I go to a photocomposition house (a typesetter) with a page full of the words I need. I have them set in a typeface I like, in sizes appropriate to the size drawing I will prepare. Many other architects—and most students—use transfer letters laboriously rubbed down for each sheet's title block. I've done that and find it boring and repetitious, and therefore I make mistakes. I also always run out of a single letter before the end. When I have my type, I Xerox it onto stick-on transparent flexible film like Stan-pat and make several title blocks at one time. I also frequently letter titles by hand, especially on early design studies.

CHAPTER FIVE

AXONOMETRIC DRAWINGS

The plan, section, and elevation drawings described in Chapter 3 are fundamental to architecture. Even when intended exclusively for presentation purposes, and therefore not given the dimensional detail and notes of more developed drawings, they have a precision that lets them stand in for the building or object they represent. They "feel" right and are very reassuring. But the feeling of reassurance they give is sometimes limited to architects and designers; to most of the public they are technical drawings. Another kind of drawing, more closely related to the way people see, is needed for full communication.

Seeing is a dynamic process. Even when our bodies are still, our eyes are in motion. We get multiple views of what we see, and most of those views are oblique. By that I mean we look at much of what we see from other than a head-on angle and have two, three, or more faces of the object revealed to us at one time. The drawings we have studied to this point are single view in that they provide information about only one face of their subjects.

Oblique views are essential to us for depth perception, which in turn informs us of the real size of objects and of their location in space relative to ourselves. This information allows us to know where we stand; it places us in the world. I believe there is a fundamental human need to know, through the eyes, where we are. Once that knowledge is available, the mind can go on to other higher functions.

We are most comfortable with an oblique view of virtually any three-dimensional object since that view provides more of the sort of relational information the brain needs. This comfort must be regarded as precious by those who design new things—we design for people and need to have them understand our designs.

There are two large classes of oblique views available to architects and designers. They are "perspective" views and "axonometric" views. Axonometrics (the root words mean "measurable along the axes") are also frequently referred to as "paraline" drawings. They are relatively easy to make, once you have grasped the underlying ideas. Axonometric views give a "fake" perspective in that they create the illusion of an oblique view without obeying all the laws of optics and without the fuss of construction that perspective involves. These are the quintessential "bird's-eye views," although other angles of view are possible.

The most natural and widely used of the oblique views is the perspective. Perspective drawing strives to recreate all the relational information that reality provides and accurately renders optical phenomena. This additional information, described in Chapter 6, makes them the most readily understood drawings by our viewers. However, axonometrics, like perspectives, do reveal several faces of an object at one time, and this fact alone is apparently enough to make them convincing. Since they are substantially easier to construct than perspectives, they are frequently a speedy and simple alternative.

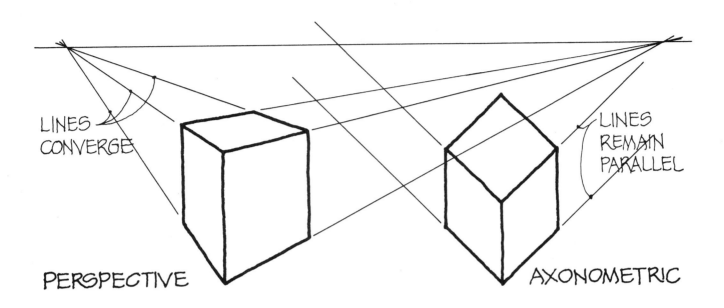

FACTORS COMMON TO ALL AXONOMETRIC DRAWINGS

All axonometric drawings include three axes that correspond to width, depth, and height. Each line drawn parallel to these axes is scalable, meaning that it can be measured with a scale throughout its length. (Not all axonometric drawings use the same scale on each axis, however; see below.) Angles used to construct axonometric drawings follow conventions that usually correspond with the built-in angles of triangles, making the construction of an axonometric drawing fairly simple. (Where there is an angle in the object—such as at a bay window—it needs to be found by geometric means in the constructed axonometric. A method for doing this is shown below.)

AXONOMETRIC CATEGORIES

There are several axonometric drawing categories, and the differences between them are not always well understood today. I suspect that this is because the teaching of drawing in design/architectural schools, once central to curricula and a required precursor to further design education, was neglected for about 25 to 35 years in this country. The descriptive words have survived, but they have fallen into popular usages that may be deceiving. I will try to sort them out.

1. The whole group is called "axonometric," which simply means "dimensionable along the axes," as mentioned earlier.

2. A drawing of a building or object viewed obliquely that includes angles of 90° between any two adjacent walls (that is, like the one described in the sequence of steps on pages 72-76) is often popularly called "axonometric."

3. If instead of a 90° angle between adjacent walls the obliquely viewed object includes 120° between its right and left front walls, the drawing is an isometric. This type of drawing is as popular as the axonometric, and its construction will be detailed in another step-by-step sequence below.

4. The word "isometric" means "equal measure" and is derived from the theory of isometric projection that underlies this drawing category.

5. If the object were drawn with two different scales so that distances along the front plane were shown true to scale and those along the receding planes were shown, for example, at two-thirds the scale of the front plane, a false diminution would be produced. Diminution is one of the principal characteristics of perspective drawings that is missing from axonometrics unless it is induced in some artificial way (such as by using two different scales). A drawing of this type is called "dimetric," for "two measures." Such drawings were once very popular, and the study of them was a part of every student's schooling. They are not common today.

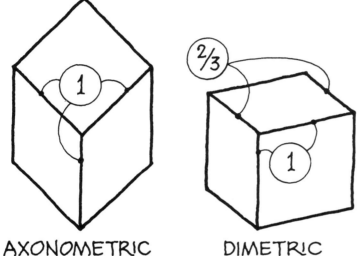

AXONOMETRIC   DIMETRIC

6. There is another drawing type, not strictly an axonometric at all, which is called "oblique." This drawing is based on an orthographic view of one plane of a building—usually a facade—and an oblique view of the space behind that plane. The drawing type is labeled "oblique," the drawing just described a "facade oblique." I mention this drawing here because it is prepared in the same way as an axonometric, from which it differs more in theory than in substance.

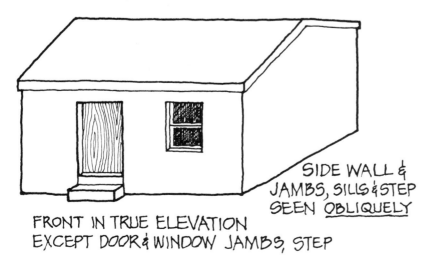

SIDE WALL &
JAMBS, SILLS & STEP
SEEN OBLIQUELY

FRONT IN TRUE ELEVATION
EXCEPT DOOR & WINDOW JAMBS, STEP

Axonometric and isometric drawings may also be constructed from plans that are not rotated (see step 1 above) by making the verticals assume an angle relative to the normal plane of the drawing, instead of making the plan do so (or in some obscure cases to lie over the lines of the plan). The latter is a somewhat recherché type of drawing, of limited use to anyone except those who are attempting to pique the fancy of architects—the general public finds the drawings quite incomprehensible. Facade obliques, on the other hand, can be very useful where you need to explain the relationship between a building's front wall and the spaces behind.

STEP-BY-STEP CONSTRUCTION OF AN AXONOMETRIC DRAWING

The simplest version of the axonometric drawing type can be made directly over the plan. It is a good one to start our step-by-step explanations with, since it is the easiest to construct and will lead logically into what follows.

1. Put a plan of your building down on the drawing board, and rotate it around the corner you want to be nearest in the final view. Stop when the sides of the plan are at exactly 45° to the long edge of your squared-up t-square. Tape down the four corners of the plan. Lay a fresh sheet of tracing paper over the plan, but orient its edges to the t-square, not to the edges of the plan underneath.

2. Make a vertical line on the new paper at the inside upper corner of the plan as shown. Measure with your scale (same one as for the plan!) the exact height of the room or object you are drawing along this new line from where it begins in the corner. Make a tick mark at the measured height.

TICK MARK AT CEILING HEIGHT

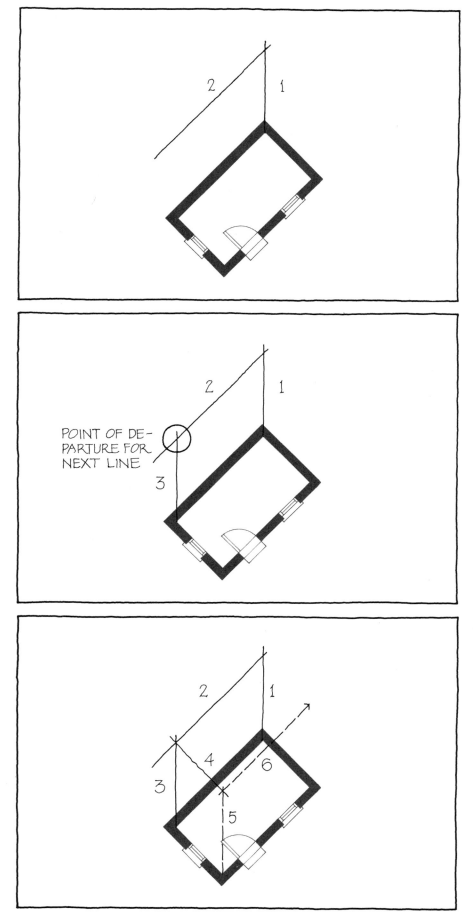

3. With your 45°-45°-90° or adjustable triangle starting at the tick mark, make a line that runs parallel to one of the floor edges. Make the line long enough to reach the next corner.

4. Make a vertical line at this next corner long enough to reach the line you just made in 3 above. Note that each time two lines intersect they give you a point of departure for a new line. This fact is fundamental to architectural drawing.

POINT OF DE-PARTURE FOR NEXT LINE

5. Make a line starting at the intersection you just created and parallel to the floor edge below. Draw in the next vertical line and the next diagonal.

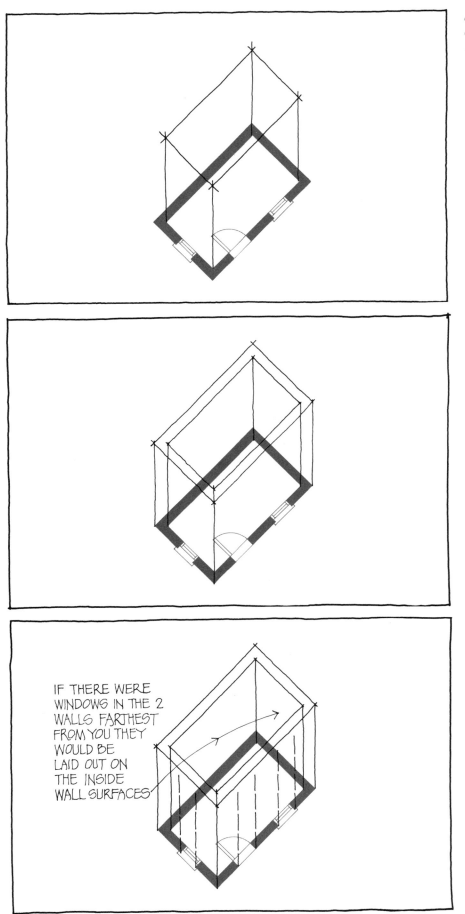

6. Make the final vertical and the last diagonal. You have completed the outline of the room's ceiling plane.

7. Now follow the same procedure for the four outside corners.

8. Using your t-square and triangle, make shorter vertical lines wherever windows and doors occur in the plan. As a general rule, these lines should be made on the outer surface of the two walls nearest the viewer and on the inner surface of the other two walls.

IF THERE WERE WINDOWS IN THE 2 WALLS FARTHEST FROM YOU THEY WOULD BE LAID OUT ON THE INSIDE WALL SURFACES

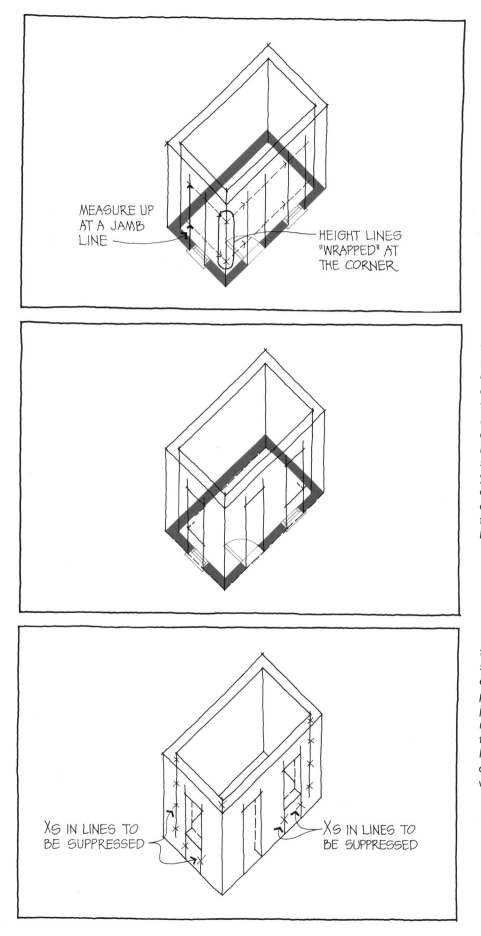

MEASURE UP
AT A JAMB
LINE

HEIGHT LINES
"WRAPPED" AT
THE CORNER

Xs IN LINES TO
BE SUPPRESSED

Xs IN LINES TO
BE SUPPRESSED

9. Measure up along any of these lines to the height of the window heads. Make a tick mark. While you're there, measure along the same line to the height of the sills, and make a tick mark. Draw the lines that will be the window heads and sills through these tick marks parallel to the floor and ceiling lines in that wall. If you continue these lines to a corner and make tick marks there, you can flip your triangle over and continue making window head and sill lines on the wall plane adjacent to the one you started on. In this way you can "wrap" measurements around at least two planes of the building or room.

10. The drawing is getting cluttered up with lines at this point, and the plan underneath is beginning to add its own confusion. Before you remove it, however, you might as well take any additional data off it you can. In this drawing the short lines that represent the corners of the door and window cutouts have been drawn. Note that since these short lines are perpendicular to the wall you are drawing, they are parallel to one of the three major axes. Don't abandon the system here! The lines of the floor-to-wall-plane join have also been drawn in.

11. Take out the plan underneath, and tape your axonometric back down. It's still a bit confusing, and there are some extra lines that we need to remove (suppress). First, though, finish the window jamb lines. At this point I like to take a red pencil and make large Xs through the lines I don't want. That helps me later when I am tracing this drawing and the tracing paper has cut down on what I can see of the original.

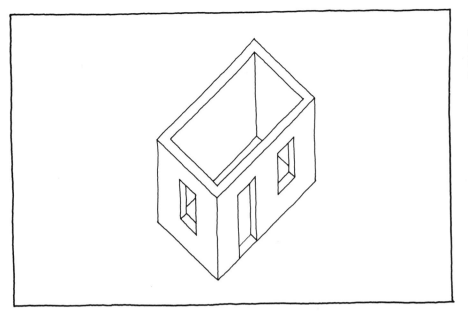

12. Lay a fresh sheet of vellum over the drawing you've been working on, and start your final presentation drawing. Follow the conventions for choosing line weights given in Chapter 4.

CONSTRUCTING AN ISOMETRIC DRAWING

The second major category of axonometric drawing is called "isometric." The name is derived from the theory underlying this drawing type (that is, the axonometric projection) and means "equal measure." For our purposes, isometrics may be thought of as purely constructed drawings, by which I mean that no part of them is traced, as the plan is, for example, in an axonometric drawing. They therefore involve somewhat more effort to produce than axonometric drawings. However, they are not very hard to make and can give a somewhat less distorted or warped sense of an object than the axonometrics, which can seem to twist large objects or buildings. The appearance of an isometric is quite different from that of an axonometric: the latter emphasizes roof or top planes, whereas the former emphasizes facade walls.

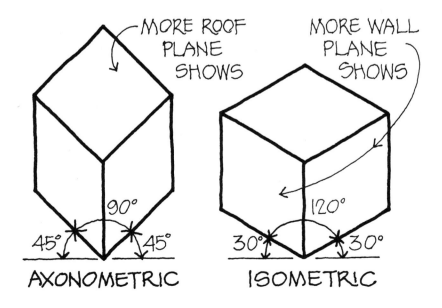

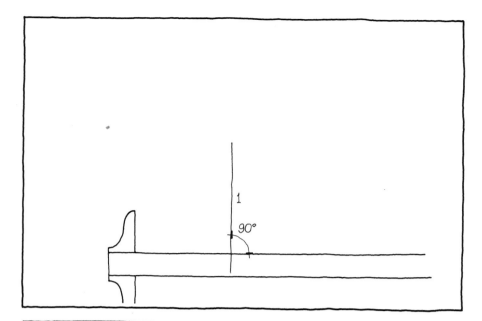

1. As always, start by assembling the materials and information you will need. In this case that means a plan and a section or elevation if they are available. It is also very helpful to have a 30°-60°-90° triangle for this drawing. Lay a sheet of working-out paper on your drawing board, and tape down the edges. Toward the front (near your belly) and approximately where you want the nearest corner of the final drawing to be, make a vertical line about as long as the walls of your object are high.

2. At the bottom of that line, make a line running up and to the right at 30° angle to the t-square. This line should be approximately as long as the right-hand wall-floor join line. Where line 2 began, make a third line that goes up and to the left at a 30° angle to the t-square. The three lines just made are the three axes of your drawing and the beginnings of the isometric.

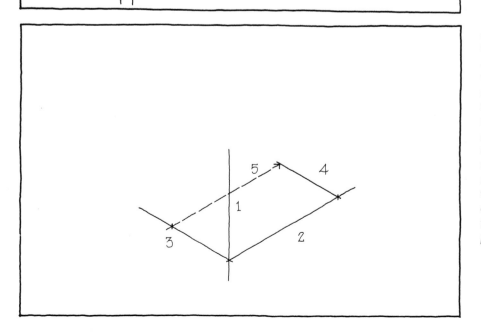

3. With your scale (same one as used for the plan), lay out the length of the right-hand wall along the right-hand wall-floor line. Make a tick mark where it ends. Now make a line starting at that tick mark that goes up and to the left at an angle of 30° to the t-square. Measure along the left-hand wall-floor line (or along line 3 you made earlier) the length of the left-hand wall, and make a tick mark. Draw in a fifth line with your triangle that connects lines 3 and 4 and that runs through this last tick mark. You have completed the base perimeter of your object in isometric.

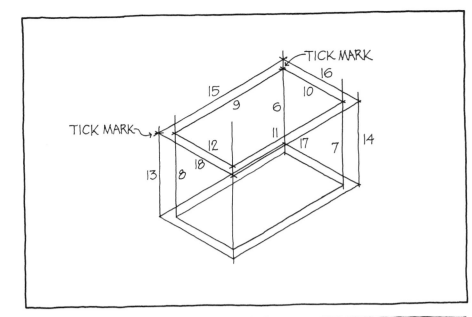

4. At each intersection draw a vertical line approximately as long as your object is high. Measure up along one of these verticals, and make a tick mark at the appropriate height. Using your 30°-60°-90° triangle, lay out the ceiling lines. Now do the outside walls in the same way as you have done the inside.

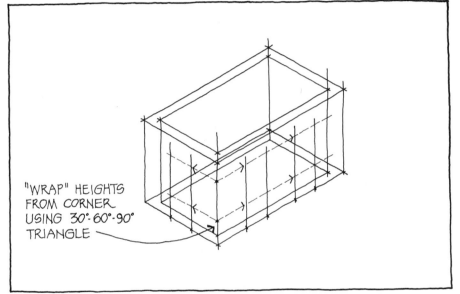

"WRAP" HEIGHTS FROM CORNER USING 30°-60°-90° TRIANGLE

5. In the same way now measure the appropriate distance along each wall (the distance is taken with a scale from your plan), and make tick marks for each window or door. Using a triangle, carry these tick marks up the walls. Measure up with the scale along any one of these new verticals (since they are parallel to one of the three axes, you may measure on them) to where the window heads and sills occur. Make the appropriate lines.

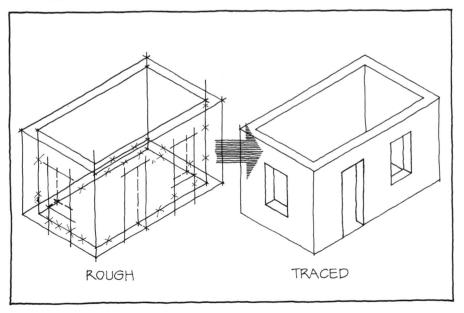

ROUGH   TRACED

6. Finish the drawing by continuing in much the same way as you did for the axonometric. Mark all lines that will not be visible in the final version with an X or some other mark (I use a red pencil for this). Lay a sheet of vellum over your construction, and trace the final presentation drawing.

ODD ANGLES IN AXONOMETRIC AND ISOMETRIC DRAWINGS

Odd angles sometimes occur in buildings—as, for example, at bay windows—and it can be confusing to draw them in the axonometric and isometric views we have described. Drawing them involves wrapping the odd-angled object with a box that follows the main wall directions of the plan. It will look as though you are adding an extention to your plan. The box is projected into the axonometric just as though it were part of the plan. Draw it lighter than the plan since the next step involves plotting points along the sides of the box that correspond to the corners of the odd-angled object. Since the box added to the drawing appears only faintly, I think of it as a "phantom" box. As was mentioned in the step-by-step axonometric sequence, points of intersection give us points of origin for new lines. In this case the new lines are vertical.

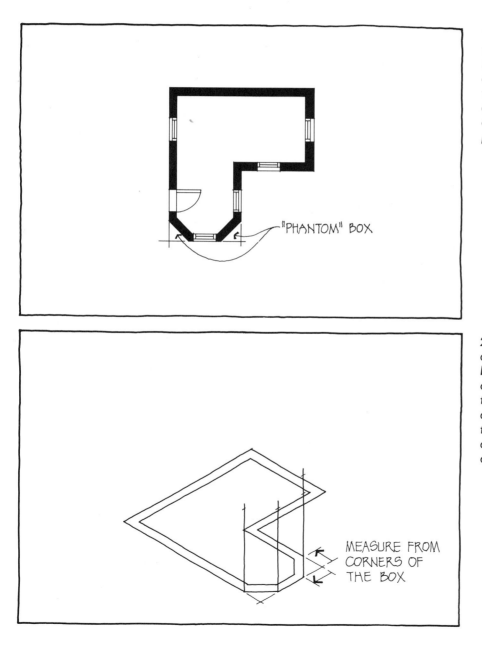

"PHANTOM" BOX

MEASURE FROM
CORNERS OF
THE BOX

1. On the plan of the building or object with the odd-angled part, lay out a square or rectangle around the odd-angled portion. It should touch the various faces of the odd-angled piece and be drawn parallel to the main axes of the plan. You can think of this as the phantom box.

2. Set up and draw the isometric as described above, including the phantom box. Scale off the distances from the corners of the box to the points where the vertical intersections of the odd-angled portion are located on plan. Lay those distances out in the isometric, and draw in the vertical intersections of your odd-angled portion.

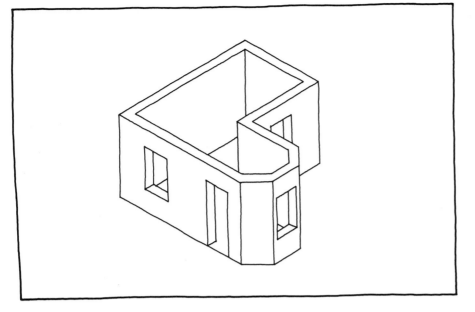

3. Complete the drawing as already described.

CIRCLES IN AXONOMETRIC AND ISOMETRIC DRAWINGS

Possibly the most confusing thing to draw in oblique views is a circle in plan. Strictly a circle in plan remains a circle in an axonometric drawing; since all plan pieces are projected unchanged, so will circles be. But they look very strange. On the premise that a circle seen obliquely will always be an oval (or more properly, an ellipse), many people modify their circles in axonometric drawings in the interest of a more natural appearance. In isometrics circles always become ellipses, so let's proceed to them.

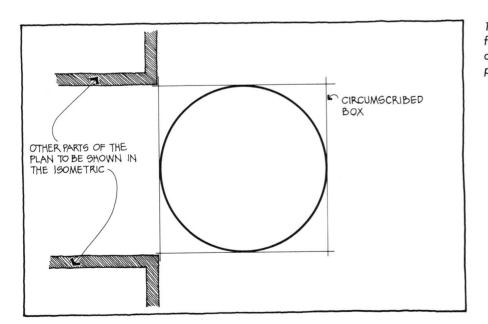

CIRCUMSCRIBED BOX

OTHER PARTS OF THE PLAN TO BE SHOWN IN THE ISOMETRIC

1. To draw a circle in an isometric, the first thing you must do is place a box around the circle in plan. Make its sides parallel to the two axes of the plan.

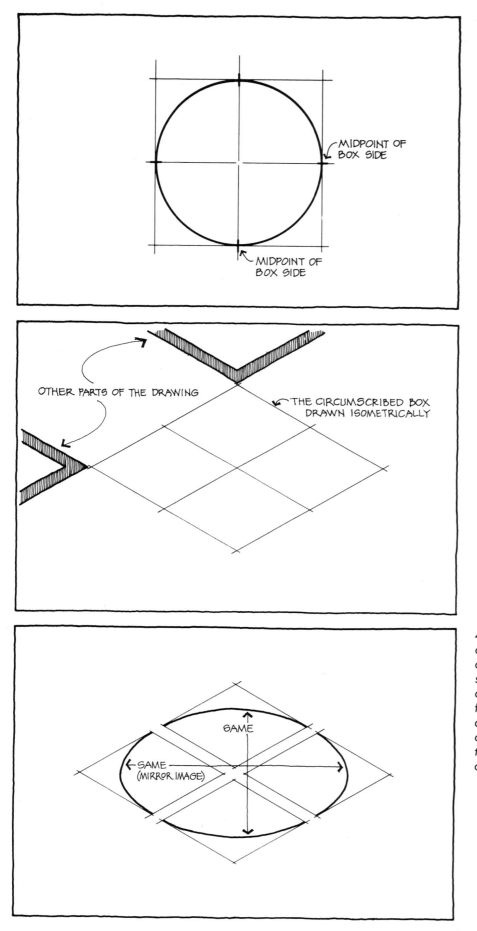

2. Subdivide the box into four equal boxes by drawing lines at the midpoints of the sides to join parallel sides.

MIDPOINT OF BOX SIDE

MIDPOINT OF BOX SIDE

3. Now locate that box in your isometric drawing just as you would any other object that paralleled the main axes of the drawing. Include its subdivisions.

OTHER PARTS OF THE DRAWING

THE CIRCUMSCRIBED BOX DRAWN ISOMETRICALLY

4. When a box is inscribed around a circle, four points of tangency are created. They occur at the midpoints of the sides of the box. If those midpoints are connected with straight lines to create four "little" boxes, each will contain an arc that represents one-quarter of the circle. In an ellipse those arcs are distorted, but they remain symmetrical diagonally across the box.

SAME

SAME (MIRROR IMAGE)

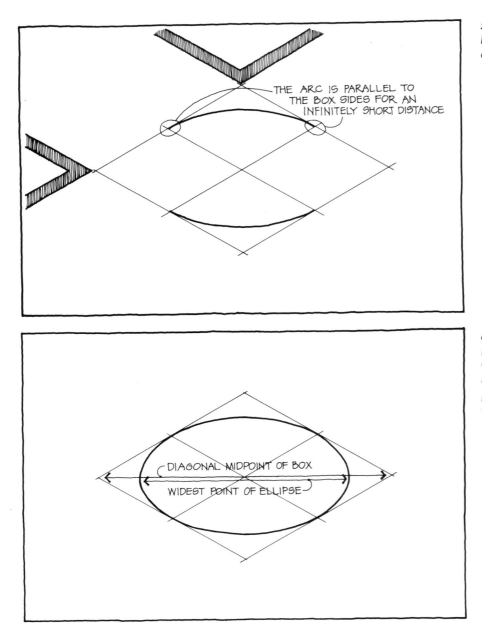

THE ARC IS PARALLEL TO
THE BOX SIDES FOR AN
INFINITELY SHORT DISTANCE

DIAGONAL MIDPOINT OF BOX

WIDEST POINT OF ELLIPSE

5. Start drawing your circle freehand beginning with the shallower pair of arcs.

6. Complete the circle by drawing in the more pointed pair of arcs. Note that the widest point of the ellipse you have just created should be in front of the mid-point of the box. This coincides with optical phenomena the eye expects and makes the ellipse credible as a circle in "perspective."

CHAPTER SIX

GENERAL INTRODUCTION TO PERSPECTIVE

The chapters that follow break down the study of perspective drawing into manageable parts. Chapter 6—this chapter—provides a general introduction to the subject, to its elements and terms. Information found here is applicable to all perspective drawings.

Chapters 7 and 8 are devoted to the step-by-step process of constructing one- and two-point perspectives. Perspective drawing is divided into categories based on the number of vanishing points used to make them. Vanishing points are defined later in this chapter. The main categories are one-point, two-point, and three- or more point. One- and two-point make up 95 percent of what architects and designers need to draw, and so they will be explained here. Three-point perspective is a sort of two-point extravaganza, making use of all its properties—and theory—and adding only another vanishing point. Three-point perspective is useful where extremes to elevation are needed, as in bird's-eye views of tall buildings. It is necessary so seldom that it has been omitted in favor of more frequently needed information. The Selected Bibliography includes several books that teach three-point.

Chapters 7 and 8 will also assist you in laying out the line "frames" of your drawings (which will be explained in detail there).

Chapter 9 contains a step-by-step sequence for drawing furniture in either one- or two-point perspective, though this technique is fundamentally the same as that used for laying out the perspective frames. Chapter 9 also includes information on how to select viewpoints, on enlarging or diminishing the size of the final drawing, and on drawing circles in perspective.

It is important to remember that perspective drawing strives to conjure up in the mind of the viewer an impression of the built design. As such, it is intentionally propagandistic. Rendering of the drawing—the addition of textural and lighting detail—is therefore frequently critical. You should review Chapter 4 as you consider how to complete your drawings.

PERSPECTIVE IS HOW WE SEE . . .

Perspective drawings are another category of oblique views. They closely approximate much of our seeing and therefore are most understandable to viewers. Quite in addition to their value as tools for communication with others is their value as tools for the design process.

Perspectives give us information about our designs in directly perceivable form that orthographic drawings simply cannot. Once you have learned to make perspectives, you will find that they become easier with practice, and soon you will make rough perspective drawings as design study aids. Eventually, your freehand perspective sketching will improve from the study of constructed perspective. That is because the rules are the same, and knowledge of one informs the other.

Perspectives differ from axonometrics in that they offer an infinite range of choice for locating the vantage point the view is taken from. This makes them a more versatile tool than axonometrics.

There are additional differences. Perspectives add three properties to those of axonometric views: convergence, diminution, and foreshortening. These properties make the perspective realistic where the axonometric is stilted and artificial.

Convergence is the tendency of parallel lines moving away from the viewer to appear to get closer to one another until they seem to merge—and ultimately vanish.

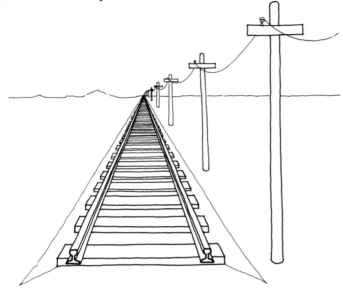

Our knowledge of the world tells us this isn't so, but we see it happen all the time. In fact, when we don't see it, things look skewed—as they do, for example, in an axonometric drawing.

Diminution is possibly the most necessary of the attributes of perspective. It refers to the fact that objects appear to become smaller as they are farther away from us.

A ROW OF LOCKERS

The brain interprets this fact into all kinds of other knowledge: how far away something is, what its relationship is to other objects in the field of view, and so forth.

Foreshortening is the compression and change in apparent geometry that occurs when an object is rotated in our field of vision. Think of a pencil or a book turned to an oblique angle in relation to your face. The pencil loses length, the book height.

DIMENSIONS IN THIS
PLANE ARE FORESHORTENED

Superimposition is an equally important visual clue, but it is an artifact of composition, not an inherent optical quality. Superimposition is the layering of object over object in our visual field. It serves to give us important depth information, which in turn helps us determine size data for unfamiliar objects.

These characteristics of perspective are part of the relational information needed by the human brain that we discussed in the last chapter. They make perspectives essential drawings in most presentations.

Regrettably, perspective is the part of design drawing that is the hardest for most students (and, for that matter, most designers) to master. In fact, if taken step-by-step, it is not so terribly hard to learn. It is based on a small number of rules first systematized in the 15th century. These rules are founded in the laws of optics and amount to the codification of what we already know through our eyes.

A big problem in learning perspective seems to be that it involves more steps—more construction—than our other drawings. Moreover, most of us make many fewer perspective drawings than orthographic drawings, so we forget the steps involved in perspective construction. Textbooks on drawing generally rely on a few horribly complex drawings that contain every line and point needed along the way, all neatly labeled. What we need, however, is something that untangles all those lines, that builds up the perspective in easy stages. That is what the following chapters do.

To further confuse and compound matters, there are several ways to construct perspectives. Though they are all variants on a theme, you may find that your classmates know a little, or even a lot, about an easier or quicker method than the one shown here. I don't insist on this method with my students. It *is* the method that I have had the greatest success teaching with and that lingers in the minds of my students. It explains the underlying visual laws. Anything that helps you understand and master perspective drawing is legitimate as far as I am concerned, so I always allow my students to construct their perspectives in any way they choose. I do suggest, however, that you maintain a healthy scepticism in the face of your classmates' judgments. The method they know, even partially, will always be faster and easier (to them) than the one that is new. Make up your own mind after first trying several ways and seeing the results.

I teach a constructed, basic, optical perspective, including no shortcuts. It will help you understand the skeleton and rules of perspective drawing and ultimately better equip you to adopt other methods.

Before we start there are some general points, applicable to all perspective systems, that we should cover.

GENERAL POINTS APPLICABLE TO ALL PERSPECTIVE DRAWINGS

There are several points that are essential to all types of perspective drawings.

1. Picture Plane. The word "perspective" comes from the Latin "see through." Understanding of perspective began with the notion of a window interposed between the artist and the subject. The subject was "seen through" that window. The artist could take a crayon and draw what he or she saw on the glass. It was a short leap from this understanding to the substitution of paper for the glass. The paper, being opaque, had to be held out of the artist's line of vision. The glass was replaced by an imaginary window, which was labeled the "picture plane" since it was in the plane of this window that the drawing was supposed to be made. Its exact corollary was that piece of paper, somewhere over there under the artist's drawing hand. They were interchangeable except for the fact that the paper was opaque. The whole concept is illustrated here.

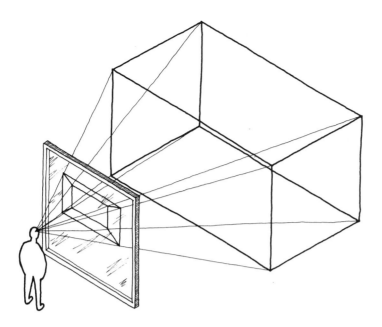

Perspective construction to this day involves the idea of a picture plane. It appears repeatedly in the diagrams that follow. Just remember: the picture plane is an idea whose real-world corollary is the piece of paper used for the drawing.

2. The Object Drawn. The next essential to all perspective drawings is the object drawn. For years the major impediment to my understanding of how perspective works was that I kept thinking that I was drawing a building or an interior. Not so. What we do is construct a perspective of and from our orthographic design drawings. The plan generates the perspective. You must learn to think of what you are doing as the projection of this very plan now on your board, not of what you have been visualizing all along. You must, for the moment, suspend your design thinking and become your own drafter—draw up what is in front of you as though it were a foreign object. Let go of thinking about its content, and look on it as pure object. Once you do that you will be well on the way to creating perspectives of what you have been visualizing all along. The verisimilitude you want, the detail and realism, are all a part of the rendering. Right now we need to pay attention to the outlines.

3. The Horizon Line. Every perspective needs a horizon line, whether it appears in the final drawing or not. The horizon line is simply the eye level of the drafter—in other words, the height of his or her eyes above the ground. It follows you wherever you go, like your shadow. Think about your view of a valley as you climb a mountain: it gets bigger and bigger. You see farther. The horizon has risen, in effect following your eyes, and thus the middleground has grown (illustrations are on the next page).

Now, by contrast, think of the (outdoor) paintings of Vermeer or his contemporaries. They lived in a flat, low country, and their paintings all have lots of sky. Put differently, the horizon is low, at eye level, about 5′ above the ground.

The horizon line is important in making perspective drawings since lines in the foreground that continue into the middle- and background all converge to a point or points on the horizon. We use the horizon line in our drawings to help locate the vanishing points.

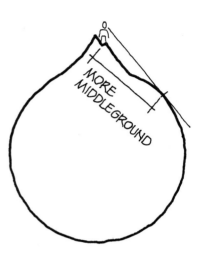

THE VIEW FROM A MOUNTAIN TO THE HORIZON. THE EARTH'S CURVATURE MUCH EXAGGERATED.

The view from a mountain ridge: note the large amount of middleground and the small amount of sky.

The View of Delft after Vermeer: note the small amount of middleground and the large amount of sky.

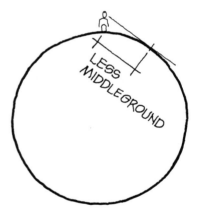

THE VIEW TO THE HORIZON IN A DESERT. THE EARTH'S CURVATURE HAS BEEN MUCH EXAGGERATED

4. The Station Point. Every perspective drawing has a viewpoint: that is, the point from which the view is made. Think of making a photograph; at the instant you press the shutter release, you freeze a picture from where you were standing. In perspective drawing the equivalent position is traditionally called the "station point"—presumably because the drafter is stationed at that point while constructing the perspective.

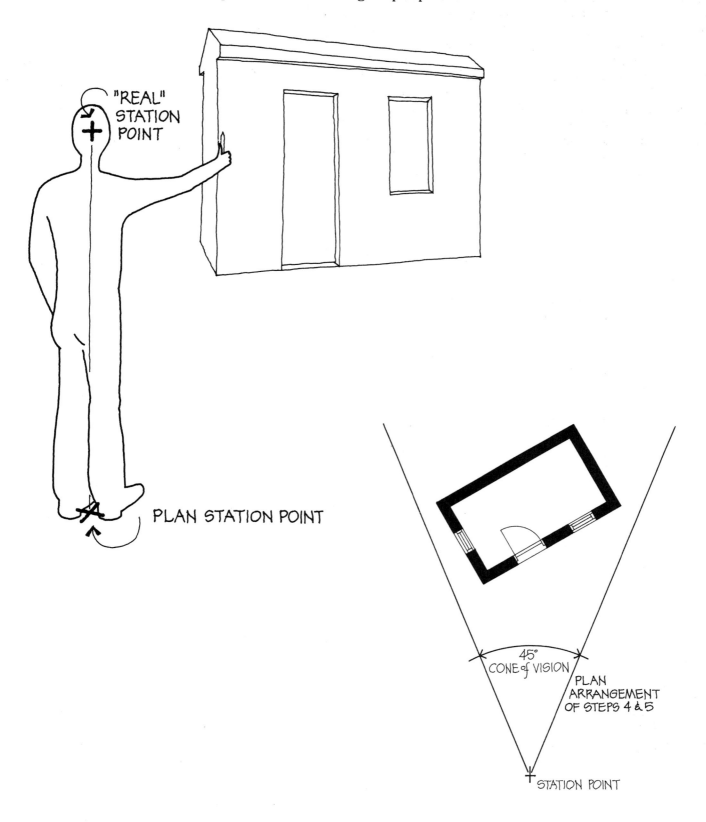

"REAL" STATION POINT

PLAN STATION POINT

45°
CONE of VISION

PLAN ARRANGEMENT OF STEPS 4 & 5

STATION POINT

5. Cone of Vision. Radiating from this station point (or eye) in the direction of the object is a field of view. It is the systematic equivalent of what the eye sees. We call it a "cone of vision," which is a useful reminder that the eye is a ball and sees both up and down and side to side. I say a useful reminder because it is easy to forget about height when you are working with plans. If you do and you are drawing a tall building that pokes through the cone of vision, you will get vertical distortion in your drawing. We'll get back to this point later when we actually set up a perspective. The cone of vision is that segment of the field of view within which an object in perspective will look right to a viewer and beyond which it will be distorted. It sets our drawing limits and is the approximate corollary of our field of view when the eye and head are held still. The need for the object to lie within the cone of vision means that the size of the object determines the size of the cone of vision, and therefore both determine the distance from the object to the station point, which is at the apex of the cone of vision.

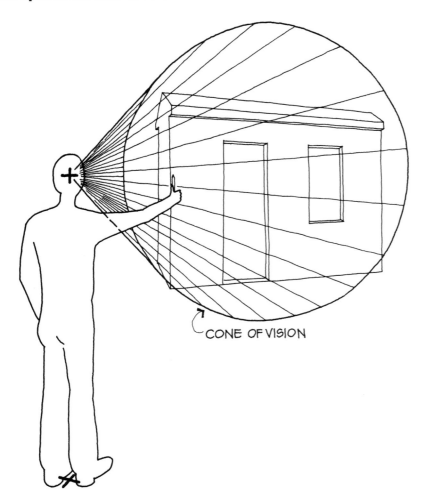

CONE OF VISION

6. Central Visual Ray. At the center of the cone of vision lies the central visual ray (CVR)—named for the rays of vision that artists in the Middle Ages thought were sent by a viewer to an object. Actually this is the center of our field of view. In a perspective drawing this line connects the center of interest to the station point. It will be most useful if you arrange your object (plan) and the station point so that the central visual ray is positioned at right angles to the t-square. It can then be drawn with a 90° triangle.

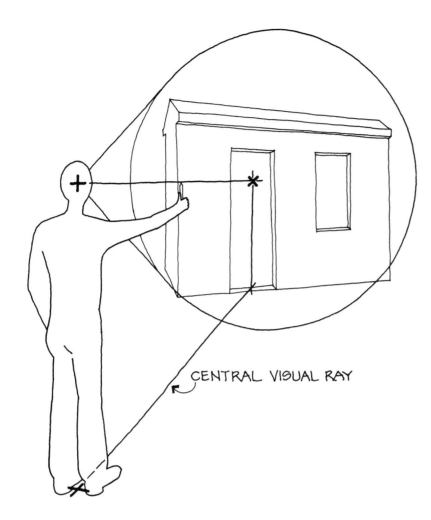

CENTRAL VISUAL RAY

7. Vanishing Point(s). All perspectives involve at least one vanishing point; this differentiates them from all the other drawings we have studied. Every set of parallel lines in a perspective drawing—except those parallel to the picture plane—converges to a vanishing point. They are usually on the horizon line since visual "rays," as they are cast at

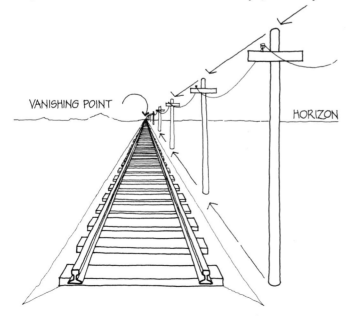

VANISHING POINT

HORIZON

ever farther objects, approach the line that represents the ray cast at the horizon. A ray cast at an infinitely far object would coincide with the ray cast at the horizon. Since most lines in our rectilinear universe are parallel to the ground, their extensions to infinity will approach and eventually meet, the horizon.

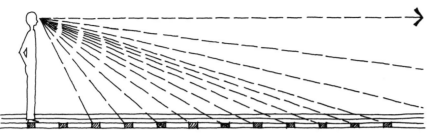

THE HORIZON IS AT VISUAL INFINITY, SO THE VISUAL RAY CAST AT IT IS HORIZONTAL...i.e., LEVEL WITH YOUR EYE!

As you start learning to make perspective drawings, you will find that you are asked over and over again to make decisions that affect the final outcome. These include: location of the station point around the plan, distance of the station point from the plan, height of the station point above the ground, location of the picture plane in relation to the plan, and possibly others. It can be frustrating to have so much freedom to exercise when you are not yet able to weigh the implications of what you are choosing. It may help you to know that even professional renderers (people who make perspectives for a living) prepare several alternate "roughs," or sketches, before deciding on a final set of parameters for a drawing.

Ultimately it may help you think back to the reasons why you set about this drawing. Is this a study perspective? If so, then what was it I wanted to study? The answer may help you determine what is the center of interest and where to locate the station point. Is it a presentation drawing? Then what is it that I most want to present? Again, the answer will help you determine approximate locations for the variables you need to control.

DON'T SPARE THE PAPER

You will be using lots of paper in drawing perspectives. Don't try not to. The paper layers separate lines and thoughts and serve as records of where you've been. The minimum number of layers is:

1. Plan (probably drawn before).

2. "Plan setup" (includes plan locations of the station point, cone of vision, central visual ray, picture plane, vanishing point or points, "rays" from the station point to every important corner or point in the plan).

3. The perspective rough (includes the initial perspective construction).

4. The final drawing (a tracing of 3 above, embellished with details and rendering).

Where a perspective drawing gets complex, involving many different plan elements in its scope, you should feel free to use as many paper layers as you think you need. Expensive as it is, paper is still cheaper than your time. The more layers you use the easier it is to keep track of what you are doing and to correct any errors you may make.

CHAPTER SEVEN

CONSTRUCTING THE ONE-POINT PERSPECTIVE

We will start studying perspective construction with one-point, which is slightly easier to set up and understand than two-point. They have a great deal in common, however, and what you learn in this chapter will be extremely helpful in the next. One-points are frequently used to reveal the interior relationships and details of dwellings and machines. One-point perspectives *by definition* place one of the two sets of rectangular organizing outlines of most plans parallel to the picture plane. The other set of lines—the one that will move into the perspective drawing—recedes to a vanishing point on the horizon somewhere within the drawing. The lines that parallel the picture plane do not converge, since they reach the horizon infinitely far from us to the right and left.

One-points require an object, a picture plane, a horizon line, an observer (standing on the station point), a cone of vision, and, of course, a vanishing point, all as defined in Chapter 6.

What follows is the step-by-step construction of a one-point perspective. Each frame will add new information to what has been laid down before. You must, if you are to benefit from this procedure, follow along with a similar step-by-step construction on your own drawing board. Read the captions, look at the frames, repeat the contents. Go back and forth to remind yourself of what you are doing (and of what you have already done).

1. Begin by collecting the information needed to draw the perspective. This includes a plan and a section or elevation. The plan is the primary "generator" of the perspective drawing and will be used throughout these steps. You must choose the best direction to make the perspective drawing from. That depends on what you want to show or emphasize about the object. Place your plan near the top of your board, so that one of its major axes (wall planes, usually) lies parallel to the blade of the t-square. Tape the plan to the drawing board. It is quite all right to allow some part of your plan to hang over the back of the drawing board as it does here. Just don't walk behind the board and crease it!

2. It may help in understanding what follows to imagine a viewer standing on your board near its front edge and looking "up" into or at the object and getting the view you have chosen. I have removed the front wall of our object so the viewer will be able to see in. What you must frequently do when you draw perspectives is make one wall transparent. This is easily done: you simply show the edges of the wall and also show whatever is behind it that would be concealed if you hadn't worked your magic.

3. Your second decision is what to make the center of interest in your drawing. This is usually the heart of a design and can be a fireplace, a furniture grouping, a bay window, or so on. The center of interest is the origin of the central visual ray in our construction. It is usually a poor idea to put the center of interest at the center of the object or of the drawing, because it makes for a static image. Place a sheet of fairly transparent tracing paper over your plan and extending below it. You will use this for the plan setup. Drop a line straight down from what you have decided is the center of interest (use t-square and triangle). This is the central visual ray.

4. The station point lies along the central visual ray. It is located far enough away so that the cone of vision it is the origin of will not be wider than about 45° and will still take in all the object. To find that point I use an adjustable triangle set to 22 1/2° and position it so that it touches the part of the plan that is farthest from the central visual ray. Where the triangle crosses the ray is the best place for the station point. Make a mark there.

5. Place the plan view of the picture plane (that is, a line) somewhere in contact with the object. For this demonstration I have put it touching the back wall of the plan. It can be anywhere you decide, but you will find (as demonstrated later) that having it coincide with a wall that is visible in the perspective is both useful and time-saving.

6. Somewhere in the portion of your new piece of paper that does not overlap the plan setup (well below it, though well within the borders of the paper), make a long horizontal line. Its location is arbitrary. This is the horizon line.

7. Using your t-square and a 4H lead to make very faint lines, connect the station point to the four corners of your object and extend these lines until they intersect the picture plane. I frequently use a colored pencil for this projection.

8. Using your t-square and triangle, drop a faint line (using either a 4H or the colored lead just discussed) straight down from each intersection at the picture plane found in 7 into the area of your perspective drawing.

9. By definition everything that touches the picture plane is shown full size. (Remember the window analogy for the picture plane and think of something moved toward it until they touch. The point of contact will be drawn full size.) Since in this setup the back wall of the subject touches the picture plane it will be shown full size. That means the full size of the wall at the scale of the plan.

10. Measure down from the horizon line 5' in the scale of the plan. Now find the lines you have brought down into the perspective that correspond to the corners the right and left side walls of the object make with its back wall, and make a horizontal line that runs between them at the 5' mark you just found. Measure up from the horizon line to ceiling height. Make a horizontal line there that ends at the right and left side walls. You have just drawn the back wall of your object in perspective. All heights in the perspective drawing will be derived from the back wall, since it is in contact with the picture plane and therefore every part of it is scalable.

11. Locate the plan position of the vanishing point through the paper layers on your board. This corresponds to where the central visual ray intersects the picture plane in your plan setup. To find it in your perspective, extend the line of the CVR with your t-square and triangle to where it intersects the horizon line established in 6. Since the vanishing point is on the horizon (by definition, see Chapter 6), the intersection of the CVR and the horizon gives you the location of the vanishing point for your perspective construction. It is simply eye level at the horizon.

12. Place a long-shanked push pin into the vanishing point, and connect it to the intersection of the floor line and the left-hand edge of the back wall. Continue this new line (it is the line where the left side of your object meets the ground or floor) until it intersects the trace of the front left corner of your object. Now do the same for the left-hand wall-ceiling join.

13. Do the same with the right-hand wall.

14. Connect the front edges of the left and right walls that you just found in 12 and 13. You have just completed the outlines of your room. You now need to project any other details of the walls or the object you are drawing.

15. If there are openings or other building elements in the walls of your perspective frame, they can be projected from the plan just as the four corners were (in 7 and 8). I use a different colored lead for the edges or corners of each separate object or opening. I find that this simple color coding helps me keep projected lines separate when I am drawing a complex object or room.

16. Now, using the 4H lead called for in frame 7, drop the intersection (often referred to as "trace") of these last lines into your perspective.

17. On the back wall, at the corner with a side wall that is nearest to the side where the opening or other building elements occurs, measure up the height of the opening (obviously in the scale of the plan). Put the push pin back in the vanishing point, and "project" the height you just measured along one or the other side wall until it intersects the lines of the opening that you dropped down in 16.

18. Now do the same for the back edge or side edge (jamb) of the opening. You need thickness in all your drawings to make them believable.

You have just completed what I think of as the perspective "frame." It is the bare bones of a drawing that now needs to have furniture and other detail added. Information on how to project the furniture is in Chapter 9, and information on how to handle the rendering generally is in Chapter 4.

CHAPTER EIGHT

CONSTRUCTING THE TWO-POINT PERSPECTIVE

On the title page of his book on perspective, first published in 1604, Jan Vredeman de Vries wrote, "Perspective, That is, the Most famous art of eyesight. . . ." He scarcely exaggerated.

We see the world in perspective. Two-point perspective is how we see it most of the time. If, as we discussed in Chapter 6, most of our seeing is oblique, then two-point perspective is the most familiar and natural of all the drawings available to designers and architects. It is the drawing that axonometrics and isometrics "want" to be. Two-point perspective frees us from the strait jackets of single views and one-point perspectives and allows us to range all around our subjects, stationing ourselves finally at the very best vantage point. This makes two-point perspective indispensable to a designer. It is the pinnacle of presentation drawing. (Three-point perspective—as explained and defined in Chapter 6—is necessary so seldom that more frequently needed information has taken its place in this book. The Selected Bibliography lists several books that teach three-point.)

This two-point perspective drawing was constructed according to the sequence of steps that follows.

Two-point is the last of the oblique views we will study in this book. Two-point perspectives require an object, a picture plane, an horizon line, a station point, a cone of vision, and, of course, two vanishing points, all as defined in Chapter 6. If you are not sure you remember what each of these is, you should look back at Chapter 6 before continuing.

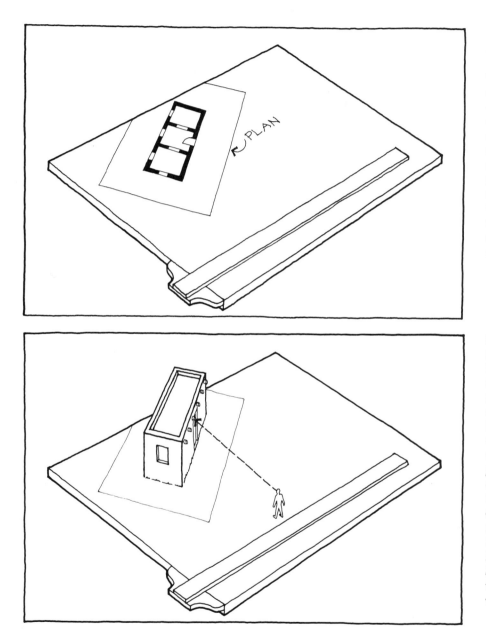

1. Begin by collecting the information needed to draw the perspective. This includes a plan and a section or elevation. The plan is the primary generator of the perspective drawing and will be used throughout these steps. Start the construction by establishing what is often called the ''plan setup.'' It consists of a plan positioned near the top of the board and includes the station point, the picture plane in plan (a line, which represents a top view of the plane), and vanishing points. We will be adding these in later steps. If you are not sure of what is meant by these terms, please read the descriptions in Chapter 6.

2. You must choose the best direction to make the perspective drawing from. That depends on what you want to show or emphasize about the object. (We will talk more about selecting a station point in Chapter 9.) It is a good idea to place your plan so much more of one of its faces shows than of adjacent one(s). This will help create a dynamic perspective. Place the plan near the top of your drawing board so its center of interest (see step 4) faces the lower edge of the board. By definition the plan must lie so that neither of its major axes is parallel to the t-square (or you would have a one-point). Tape the plan to the board. You can let some of it hang over the back edge as it does here. Just don't walk behind the board and crease it!

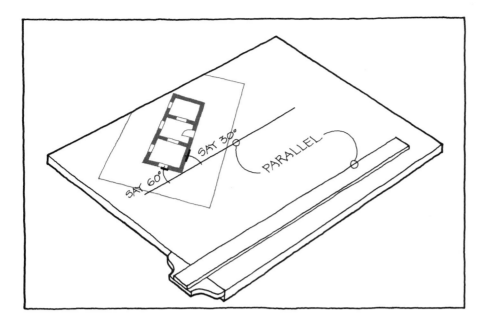

3. It may help you to understand what follows if you imagine a tiny viewer standing on your board near the front edge looking up into or at the object and getting the view you have chosen.

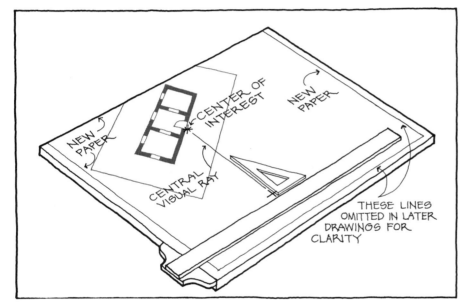

4. Your second decision is what to make the center of interest in the drawing. This is usually the heart of a design and can be a front door, a planted area, a bay window, or whatever is appropriate. The center of interest is the origin of the central visual ray in our construction. (Theoretically, it is the orthographic projection of the central visual ray onto the object.) It is usually a poor idea to put the center of interest at the center of the object or of the drawing, since doing so tends to create centripetal, static images. Place a sheet of fairly transparent tracing paper over your plan and extending below it. This layer will become the plan setup. Drop a line straight down from the center of interest (use t-square and triangle). This is the central visual ray.

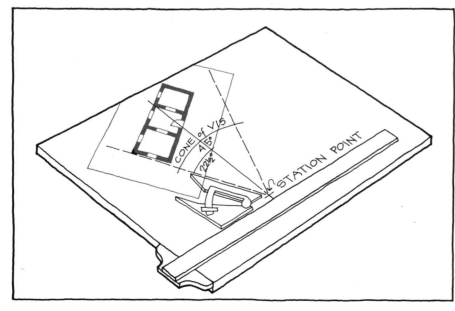

5. The station point lies along the central visual ray. It is located far enough away so that the cone of vision it is the origin of will not be wider than about 45° and will still take in all the object. To find that point I use an adjustable triangle set to 22 1/2° and position it on the t-square so it touches both the part of the plan that is farthest to the right or the left from the central visual ray and the CVR. Where the triangle crosses the CVR is the nearest nondistorting location for the station point. Make a mark there.

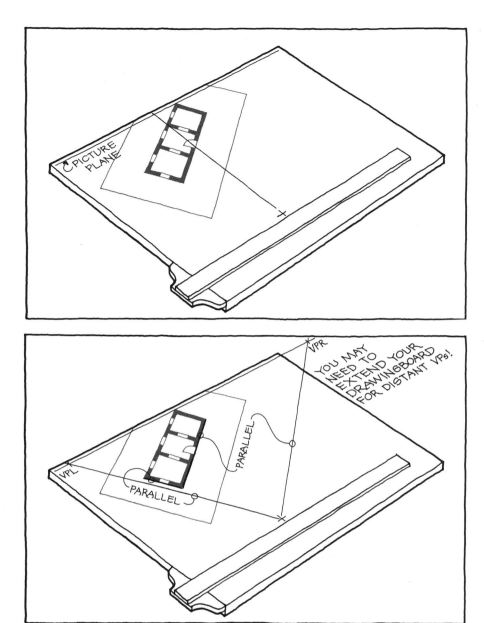

6. Place the plan view of the picture plane (that is, a line) somewhere in contact with the object. Make it with your trued-up t-square. For this demonstration I have put it touching a back corner in the plan. It can be anywhere you decide, but you will find (as demonstrated later) that having it coincide with a part of your object that is visible in the perspective is both useful and time-saving.

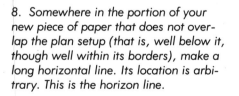

7. Make two lines starting at the station point you found in 5 that parallel the two major visible sides of your object and extend them until they intersect the picture plane you just drew. The intersections of the new lines and the picture plane are the vanishing points in the plan setup. They should be labeled VPR (vanishing point right) and VPL (vanishing point left).

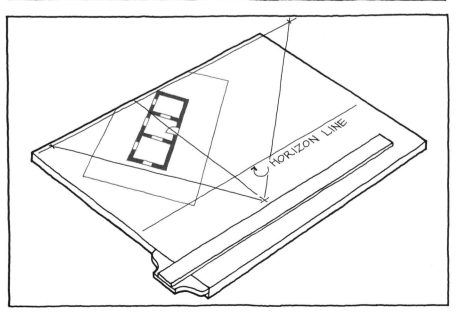

8. Somewhere in the portion of your new piece of paper that does not overlap the plan setup (that is, well below it, though well within its borders), make a long horizontal line. Its location is arbitrary. This is the horizon line.

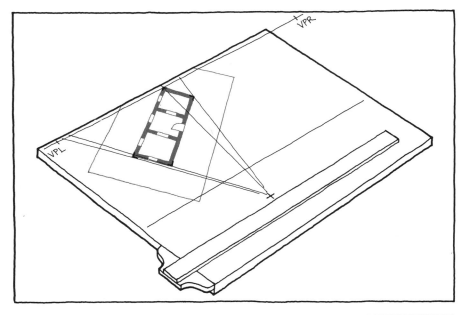

9. Using your t-square and a 4H lead to make very faint lines, connect the station point to every important point in your object, and extend ("project") these lines until they intersect the picture plane. I frequently use colored pencils instead of the 4H for this projection if there are many points. I use a different color for each "family" of important points (such as the four corners of a building).

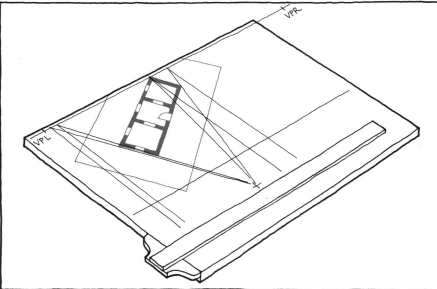

10. Using your t-square and triangle, drop a faint line (using either a 4H or the colored lead just discussed) straight down from each intersection at the picture plane found in 9 into the area of your perspective drawing. Make them long enough to cross the horizon line established in 8.

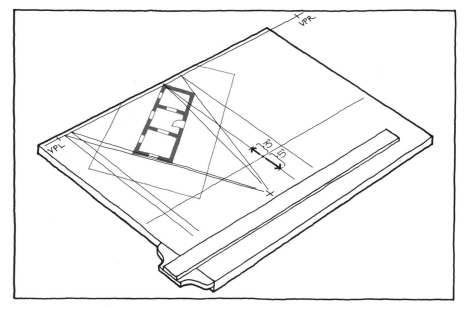

11. Since by definition everything that touches the picture plane will be shown full size (remember the imaginary window analogy and think of something moved toward it until it touches), the back corner (the one I chose in step 6) of your object will be shown in the perspective at the full size of the corner in the plan. This line becomes a "line of heights" along which we can measure heights to scale. From the point where this line crosses the horizon, measure down 5' to find the point where the line of heights touches the ground. Measure up along the same line to find the roof or top of your object.

104

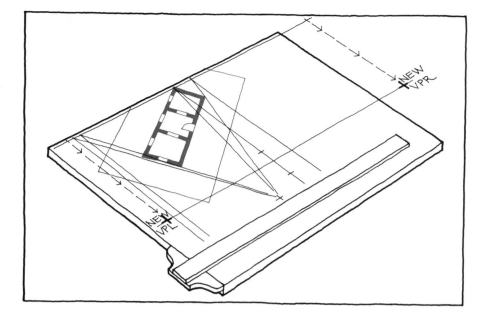

12. *Find the plan locations of VPR and VPL through the paper layers on your board. Using your t-square and triangle, drop them straight down the board into the area of your eventual perspective drawing until they cross the horizon line established in 8. These new intersections become the locii for the vanishing points in the perspective. Label them VPR and VPL.*

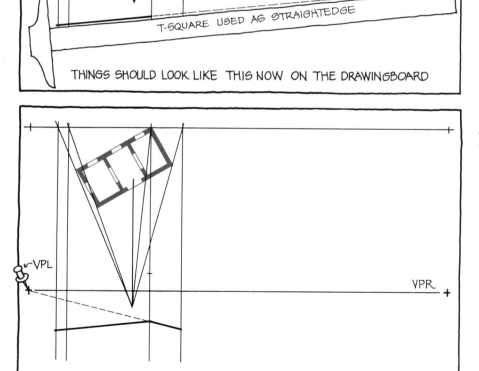

13. *Place a long-shanked push pin into the perspective VPR, and draw a line connecting it to the 5'-down mark on the line of heights. I find that the easiest way to draw these long lines is with a t-square turned upside down so its head won't latch onto the drawing board's edges. Extend this line through the tick mark until it crosses the trace of the back left corner of your object. This new line is the join between ground and the left-hand back wall of your object. The reason that lines on the left side of a drawing are sometimes drawn to a right-hand vanishing point is that they "point" to the right in the plan setup.*

14. *Do the same for the right-hand back wall of your object. You will be using VPL for this wall plane.*

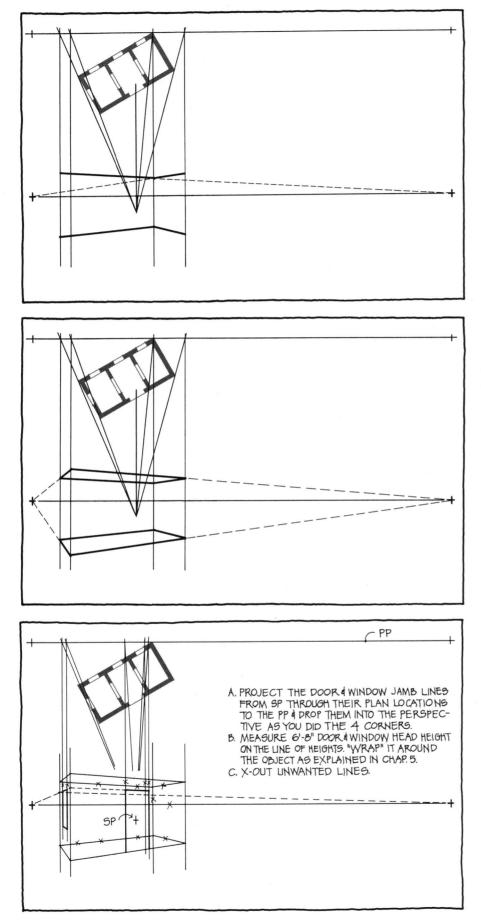

15. Now do the roof lines.

16. Where the four new lines you have drawn in 13, 14, and 15 cross the traces (the lines you brought down in step 9) of the right and left ends of the back walls, you have points-of-origin for lines that will make up the front planes of your object. Here it is the right-hand wall that can be thought of as "pointing" to the right, and that therefore is drawn with the push pin located at VPR.

17. You should have a completed block in perspective at this point. It looks transparent, since its back wall is drawn in. I like to take a colored pencil and make big Xs through the lines I won't want in the final drawing. The Xs show through the final layer of tracing paper to remind me not to trace the line.

PP

A. PROJECT THE DOOR & WINDOW JAMB LINES FROM SP THROUGH THEIR PLAN LOCATIONS TO THE PP & DROP THEM INTO THE PERSPECTIVE AS YOU DID THE 4 CORNERS.
B. MEASURE 6'-8" DOOR & WINDOW HEAD HEIGHT ON THE LINE OF HEIGHTS. "WRAP" IT AROUND THE OBJECT AS EXPLAINED IN CHAP. 5.
C. X-OUT UNWANTED LINES.

SP

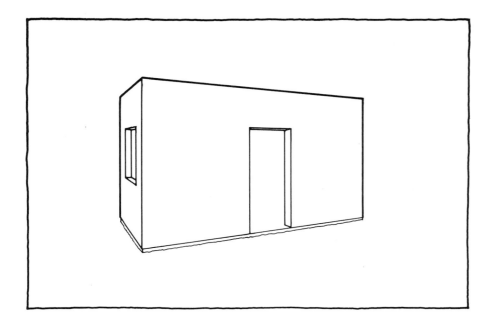

18. Lay a fresh piece of tracing paper over your perspective rough. Trace through what you want to show. Your completed tracing constitutes what I think of as a "perspective frame," since it needs embellishment before it can be a very evocative drawing.

You now have a perspective frame to embellish. The next chapter will help you with that process. The projection of furniture (both indoor and out) is a principal topic there. You will also learn various controls available to you in the construction of perspective drawings, ways to alter what is included as well as ways to adjust the station point to achieve bird's-eye and worm's-eye views.

CHAPTER NINE

DETAILS WITHIN THE PERSPECTIVE AND EMBELLISHMENTS TO IT

Now that you have learned how to make the bare bones of the perspective frame, whether that be a room in one-point or a building in two-point, you will be anxious to add details. These include furniture, cars, trees, people, and so forth. This chapter will show you ways to project your design's furnishings accurately into your perspective drawings and will explain how to make the perspective vary in size, in point of view, and in apparent realism or exaggeration of perspective effect.

LOCATING FURNITURE IN A PERSPECTIVE DRAWING

Furniture and other accessories are first projected to the picture plane from the station point in the plan setup. They are then "brought down" into the perspective. This is much the same procedure as the one we followed in establishing the perspective frames.

Before we begin, I want to suggest a new way of looking at the various objects. Perspective drawing is well adapted to the projection of points. If you can reduce an object or detail in your plan to a series of points, that object can easily and accurately be reproduced in perspective. Over the years drafters have found that the best way to do this for a complex shape such as an overstuffed armchair is by drawing in a box around each object to be shown. Then the corners of the box are projected into the perspective as the corners of the room or object were (we'll review this below), and the box is constructed in perspective. At this point the furniture can be drawn freehand into the perspective box. A complex object may require a series of contiguous boxes of varying sizes to contain it. It is fairly easy to imagine most of the furniture of our lives surrounded by a box, since boxes have come to dominate the imaginations of many post-Bauhaus furniture designers.

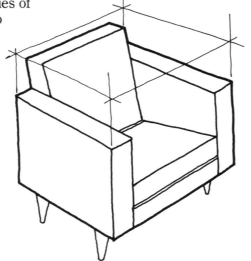

Projecting Furniture into One-Point Perspective Drawings

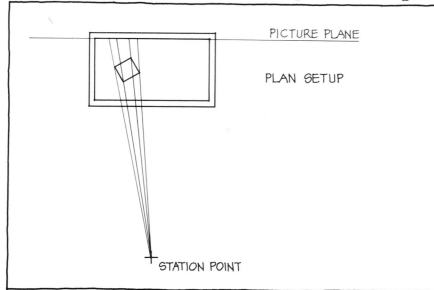

PICTURE PLANE

PLAN SETUP

STATION POINT

1. In the plan setup you have already established, draw a box around the object to be constructed in the perspective frame. The box must be snug to the object and touch its points and angles. The four corners of the box can be projected up to the picture plane if you will put a push pin into the station point, turn over your t-square, and use it to draw lines that connect the station point, the corners of the box, and the picture plane. This is the same fundamental procedure described in step 7 in Chapter 7. I use colored pencils to make the marks on the picture plane. I use a different color for each object I am projecting, which makes it easier to distinguish which marks belong to which object.

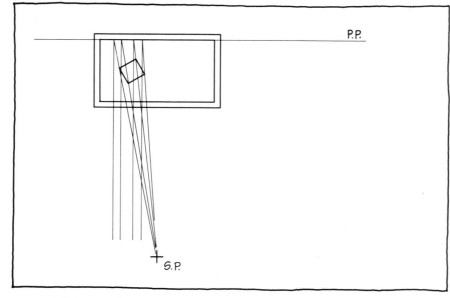

P.P.

S.P.

2. After projecting the corner points of several objects (boxes) onto the picture plane in the plan setup, bring them straight down as lines into the area of the actual perspective drawing. I use the same colored pencils for this and a t-square and triangle.

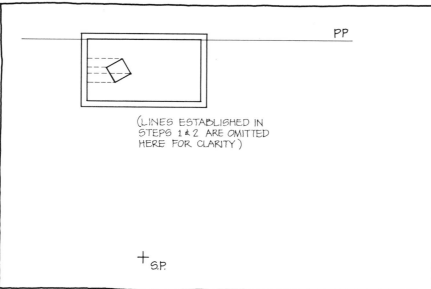

PP

(LINES ESTABLISHED IN STEPS 1 & 2 ARE OMITTED HERE FOR CLARITY)

S.P.

3. Now go back to the plan setup and "slide" the piece of furniture right or left across the room to one of the side walls. Do this by drawing a horizontal line (using the t-square) from each of the corner points to a side wall. There will be four such points if the piece of furniture is set askew in the room, but only two if it is parallel to the walls, since the back two corners will lie along one horizontal line and the front two along another.

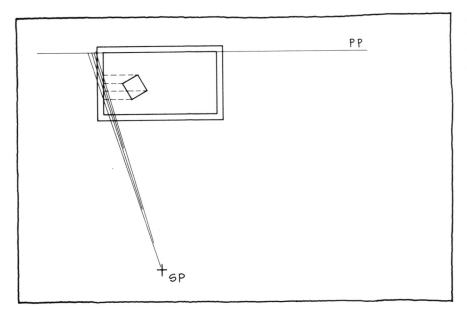

4. Using a pencil of a different color from the one used to project the four corner points in 2, project these new points (the ones found after sliding the furniture) to the picture plane. Just as you did before, insert a push pin into the station point, turn over your t-square, and use it to draw lines that connect the station point, the new points on the side wall, and the picture plane.

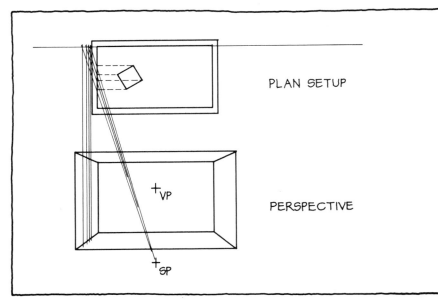

PLAN SETUP

PERSPECTIVE

5. Drop these lines straight down into the perspective (using t-square and triangle), and continue them down until they cross the line that separates the floor from the side wall. Where they cross that line is the location in perspective of the marks you made in 3 of the furniture after you slid it to the side wall.

6. Now, using the t-square, carry these new marks over into the drawing until they intersect the traces of the four corner points that you brought down in step 2. These four intersections locate the four corners of the box on the perspective's ground.

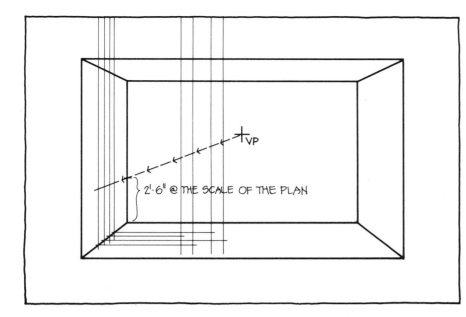

2'.6" @ THE SCALE OF THE PLAN

VP

.7. To establish the height of the box top, measure up along the back wall at the corner it makes with the side wall to which you slid the furniture. Push the push pin into the vanishing point, and (using your inverted t-square) make a line connecting it to the height mark. Continue this line along the wall. Where the height line crosses the lines brought down that wall in 5, the correct height of the box will be shown in perspective.

8. Take your t-square and carry these heights across until they intersect the traces of the furniture box corners you brought down in 2.

9. You can now construct a box within your perspective. The four corners of the bottom are connected to form a rectangle on plan. The four corners of the top are connected to form a second rectangle. The two rectangles are connected to each other. At this point I usually draw the rest of the object freehand, although you can project as many points as you will need.

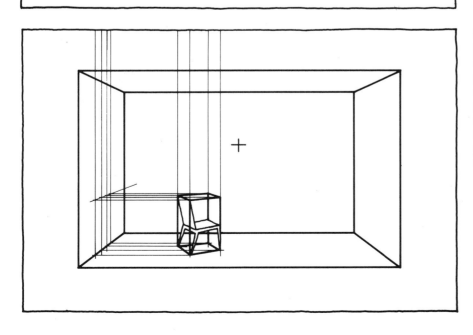

Projecting Furniture into Two-Point Perspective Drawings. The projection of furniture into two-point drawings includes "street furniture"—that is, objects in the out-of-doors or any object that doesn't conform to the ordering geometry of the major subject or building used to establish the perspective frame. In other words, the new object doesn't follow the "directions" of the old.

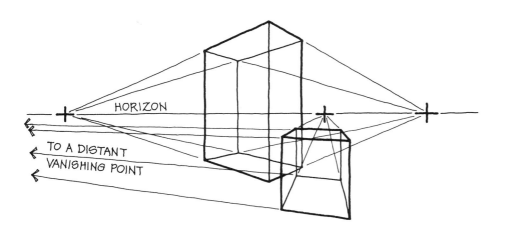

Since every set of parallel lines in a perspective drawing has its own vanishing point (review the definition of vanishing points in Chapter 6), we will set up new vanishing points for each object in the plan that doesn't conform to its main organizing geometry.

To keep our nomenclature clear, I will use the following words in the rest of this chapter:

subject = main building or object

object (or new object) = what you are projecting

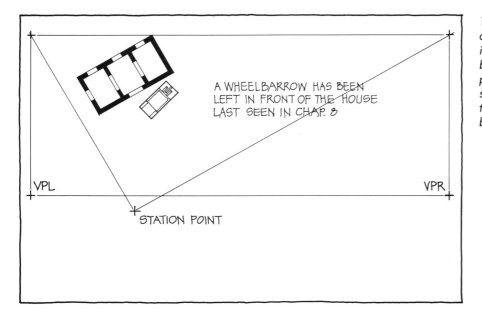

1. In the plan setup, draw a box around the object you want to project into the perspective frame. The box must be snug to the object and touch its points and angles. The sides of the box should be oriented in whatever directions allow you to comfortably fit the box around the furniture.

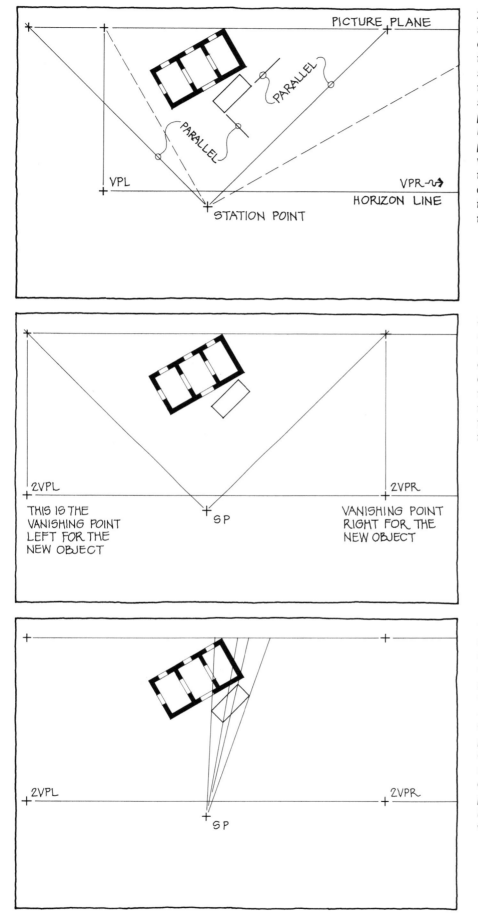

2. Establish vanishing points in the plan setup for the new box. They will be different from the ones you established for the main perspective frame since the sides of the box point to different locations on the horizon. Make two lines starting at the station point that run parallel to the two axes of the box. Extend them until they intersect the picture plane. These intersections are the vanishing-point locations of the box in the plan setup. This is the same procedure you followed in step 7 of Chapter 8 for establishing the vanishing points for the main subject.

3. Drop these new vanishing points straight down into the perspective frame using t-square and triangle. I use a colored pencil for these lines so I will be able to distinguish the new ones from the old. Where the colored lines cross the horizon is where VPL and VPR for the box are located in your perspective frame.

4. Now go back to the plan setup, and project the corners of the box to the picture plane in the plan setup. Do this by putting a push pin into the station point, turning over your t-square, and using it to draw lines that connect the station point, the corners of the box, and the picture plane. This is the same procedure described in step 9 in Chapter 8. I use colored pencils to make the marks on the picture plane. I use a different color for each object (box) I am projecting, which makes it easier to keep straight which marks belong to which object.

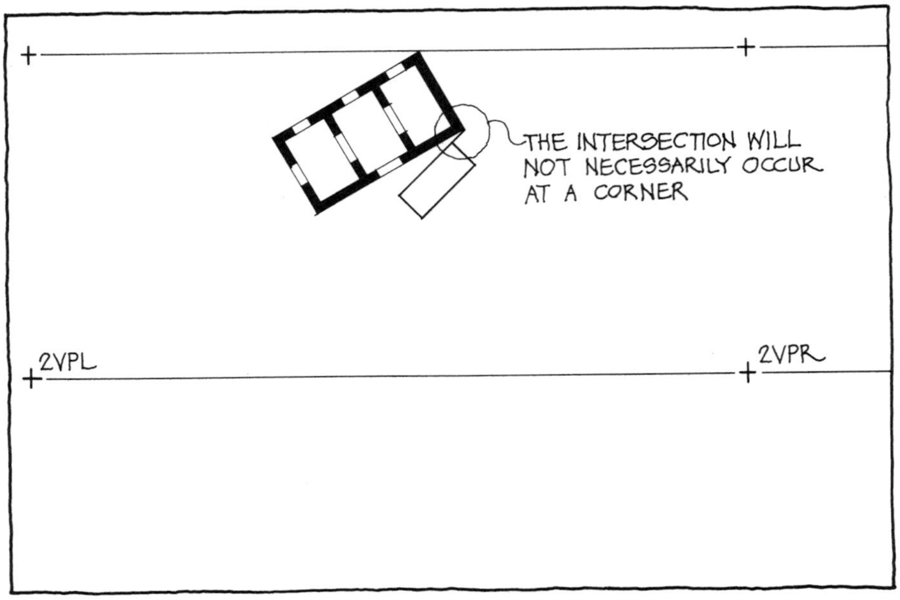

THE INTERSECTION WILL
NOT NECESSARILY OCCUR
AT A CORNER

+ 2VPL

+ 2VPR

5. While you are working in the plan setup, extend the line that forms one side of the box along its axis. Continue that line until it touches one of the major planes of the subject or the picture plane.

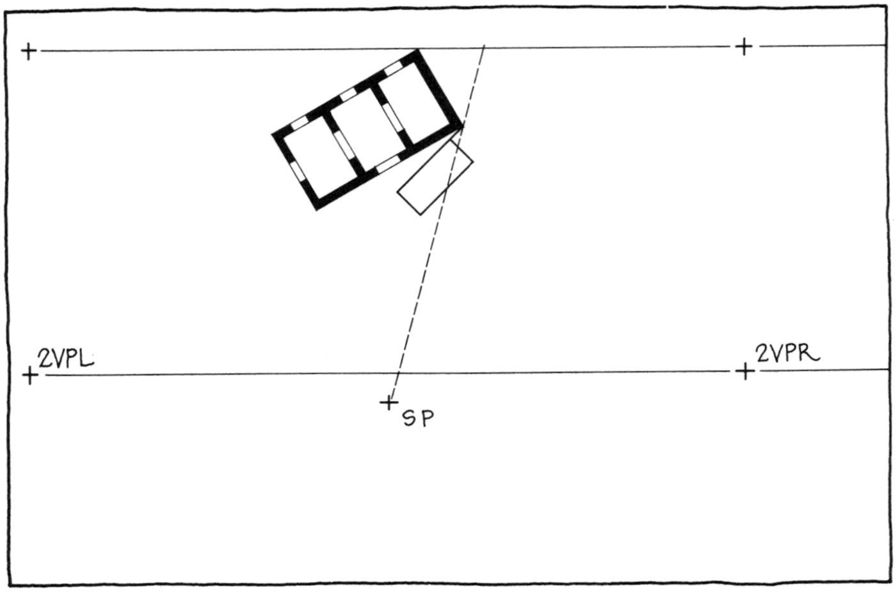

+ 2VPL

+ 2VPR

+ SP

6. Using a pencil of a different color from the one used to project the four corner points in 4, project this new point (the one found after extending the box side) to the picture plane. Just as before, insert a push pin into the station point, turn over your t-square, and use it to draw a line to connect the station point, the new point, and the picture plane.

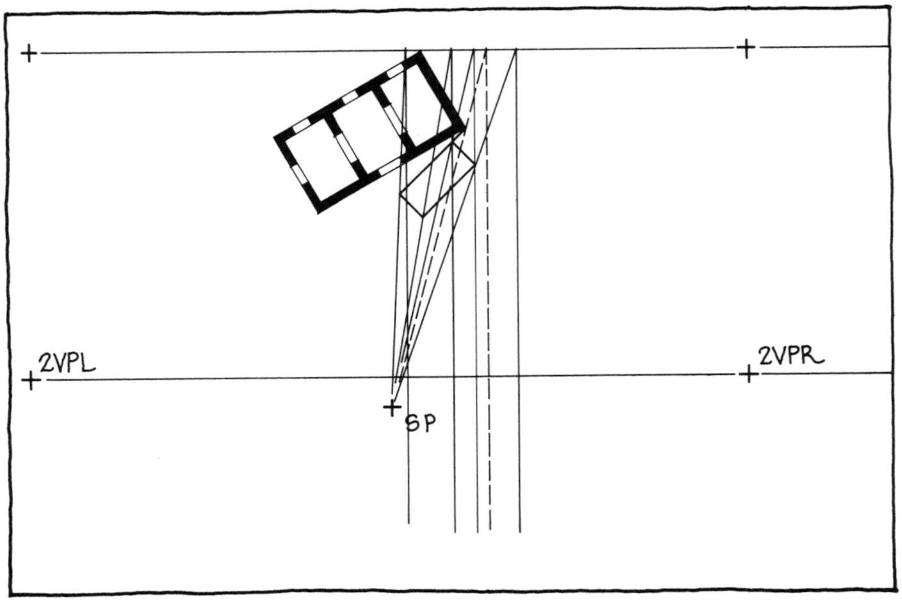

+ 2VPL

+ 2VPR

+ SP

7. Drop all these points (the four corners and the point found in 5 and 6) straight down into the perspective (using t-square and triangle), and continue them down well into the area of the ground in your perspective frame.

114

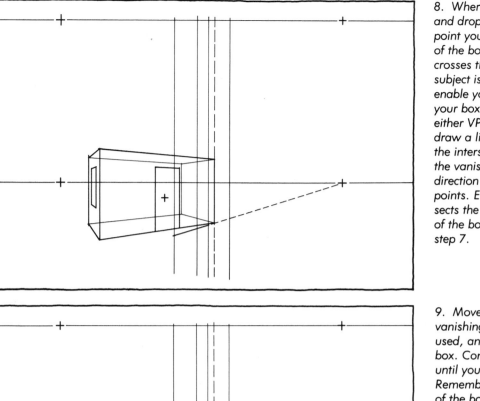

8. Where the line you projected in 6 and dropped down in 7 (the trace of the point you found by extending one side of the box until it touched your subject) crosses the ground line of the main subject is a point of departure that will enable you to draw the ground plane of your box. First, put a push pin into either VPR or VPL (for the box), and draw a line to connect that point and the intersection just described. You pick the vanishing point according to which direction the box side you will draw points. Extend this new line until it intersects the trace of one of the four corners of the box that you brought down in step 7.

9. Move the push pin to the opposite vanishing point from the one you just used, and draw the opposite side of the box. Continue moving back and forth until you finish drawing the box bottom. Remember to use the vanishing points of the box, not of the subject!

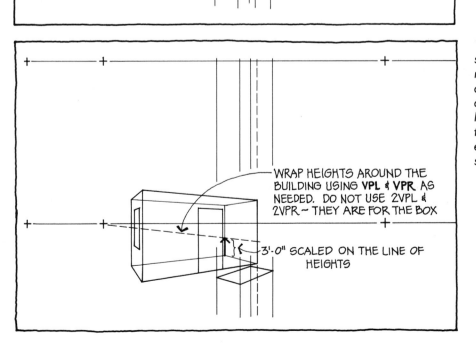

WRAP HEIGHTS AROUND THE BUILDING USING **VPL** & **VPR** AS NEEDED. DO NOT USE 2VPL & 2VPR ~ THEY ARE FOR THE BOX

3'-0" SCALED ON THE LINE OF HEIGHTS

10. On the line of heights of your main subject (see step 11 in Chapter 8), measure up the height of the box you are now drawing. Wrap that height around your subject until it intersects the line described in steps 5 and 8 (that is, the perspective trace of the line made by extending the box side until it hits the subject).

115

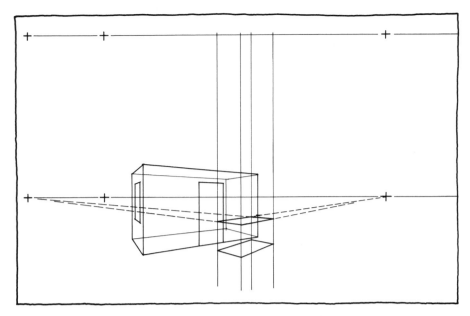

11. Project this height into the area of your box by inserting a push pin into one of the box vanishing points and projecting and wrapping as you did for the box bottom.

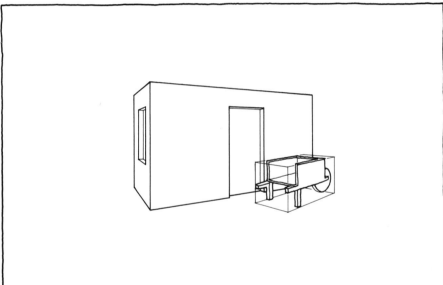

12. Connect the corners of the box bottom and top with vertical lines made with your t-square and triangle. You now have a box in correct perspective within which you can draw your furniture freehand. (Of course, you can project further points inside—or outside—the box if you need them.)

PROJECTING CIRCLES IN PERSPECTIVE

The same basic techniques that we used for projecting furniture into perspectives apply to projecting circles in perspective. Before we look at circles in perspective, however, it is a good idea to look at the geometry of a circle. A true circle (in plan) can be inscribed in a square (conversely, a square can be circumscribed around a circle). Each side of the square will be precisely as long as the diameter of the circle.

Where the circle meets the sides of the square, it is described as "tangent" to the circle (that is, parallel to it) for an infinitely short distance. This point of tangency occurs exactly at the half-way point of the square. If you draw lines connecting these half-way points across the square, you will divide it into four smaller squares and the circle within it into four quarter circles.

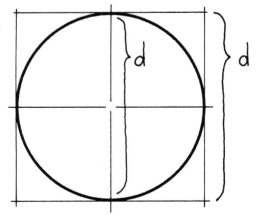

116

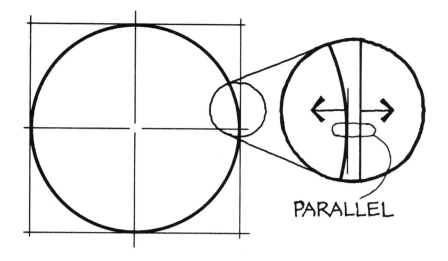

PARALLEL

This review becomes useful in projecting circles into a perspective drawing because the circular shape distorts as the eye moves to an oblique view of a circular form. Seen at any angle except head-on or edge-on, a circle looks like an ellipse. The lines of the circumscribed square are very useful in finding an ellipse in a perspective drawing.

Knowing what you now know about the geometry of circles and squares, you should be able to project a circle into a one-point perspective drawing by following the steps described earlier in this chapter for projecting furniture into a one-point drawing. Since the projection of a circle into a two-point drawing is slightly different from the projection of furniture, we will describe the new sequence here.

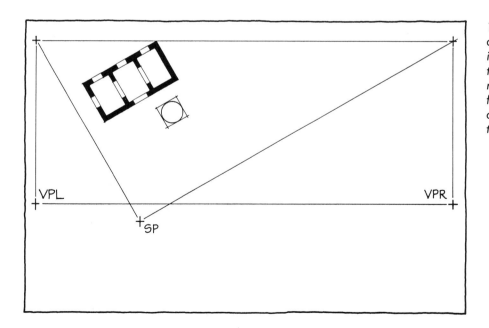

1. In the plan setup draw a square around the circle you want to project into the perspective frame. The sides of the square should be parallel to the main organizing lines of the perspective frame. The square must be snug to the circle and touch it at the four points of tangency just described.

2. Project the corners of the square to the picture plane in the plan setup. Do this by putting a push pin into the station point, turning over your t-square, and using it to draw lines that connect the station point, the corners of the square, and the picture plane. This is the same procedure described in step 9 in Chapter 8. Also as I suggested there, use different colored pencils for each square in order to distinguish which marks belong to which object.

3. While you are working in the plan setup, extend the line that forms one side of the square along its axis. Continue that line until it touches one of the major planes of the subject or the picture plane.

4. Using a pencil of a different color from the one used to project the four corner points in 2, project this new point (the one found after extending the side of the square) to the picture plane. Just as before, insert a push pin into the station point, turn over your t-square, and use it to draw a line to connect the station point, the new point, and the picture plane.

118

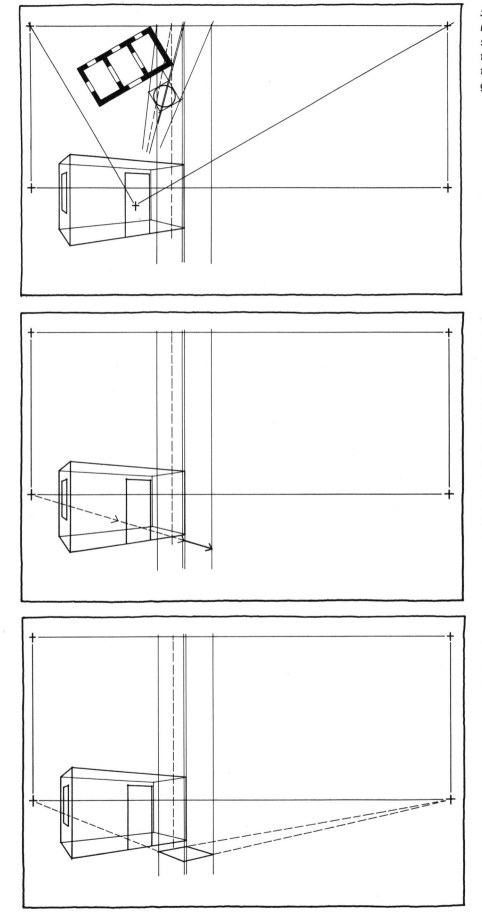

5. Drop all these points (the four corners and the point found in 3 and 4) straight down into the perspective (using t-square and triangle), and continue them down well into the area of the ground in your perspective frame.

6. Where the line you dropped down in 4 (the trace of the point you found by extending one side of the square until it touched your subject) crosses the ground line of the main subject is a point of departure that will enable you to draw your square on the ground. First, put a push pin into either VPR or VPL (for the box), and draw a line to connect that vanishing point and the intersection just described. You pick the vanishing point according to which direction the side you will draw points. Extend this new line until it intersects the trace of one of the four corners of the square that you brought down in 5.

7. Move the push pin to the opposite vanishing point from the one you just used, and draw the side on the other axis of the square. Continue moving back and forth until you finish drawing the square. Remember to use the vanishing points of the square, not of the subject!

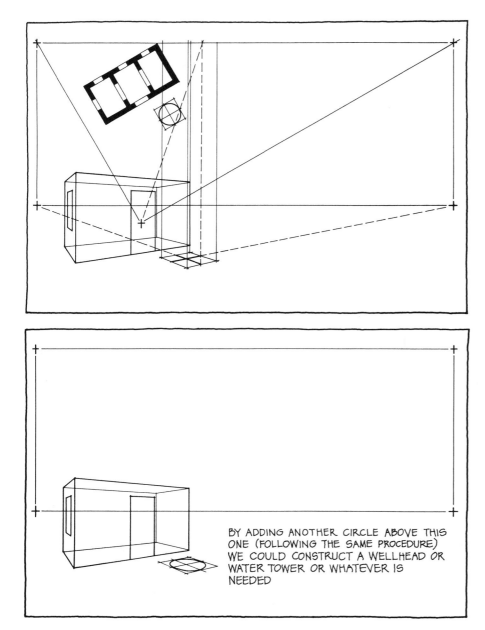

8. *Go back to the plan setup and subdivide the square into four equal squares. This involves finding the midpoints of the two front (or visible in the perspective) sides. Project these midpoints into the perspective frame and across the square as you know how to do.*

9. *Now draw your circle freehand into the framework you have just created for it. Remember that the segments of the ellipse (that is, your circle in perspective) must always meet the midpoints of the box at right angles—they are tangent to the sides at those points.*

BY ADDING ANOTHER CIRCLE ABOVE THIS ONE (FOLLOWING THE SAME PROCEDURE) WE COULD CONSTRUCT A WELLHEAD OR WATER TOWER OR WHATEVER IS NEEDED

PERSPECTIVE CONTROLS

When once you have chosen either one-point or two-point construction, there remain three fundamental variables in perspective drawing: (1) distance between the object and the station point (that is, farness or nearness of the viewer from the object portrayed), (2) position around the object in a circle of 360° (that is, its position relative to the points of the compass), and (3) height above or below the ground plane that the object rests on.

Placement of the station point (which includes all three of the variables just listed) is a fine art and one which involves the drafter in many decisions. All we can really do here is list some of the collective wisdom that architects, designers, and artists have amassed.

As we have learned in both Chapters 7 and 8, the station point should be placed so that the object viewed from it falls inside a cone of vision no wider than 45°. If the cone of vision is allowed to become wider than 45°, distortion will begin to occur at the edges of the drawing. This distortion can be quite disturbing. The drawing below will help you understand why the distortion occurs:

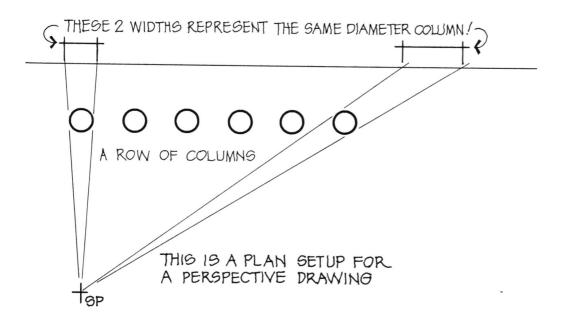

THESE 2 WIDTHS REPRESENT THE SAME DIAMETER COLUMN!

A ROW OF COLUMNS

THIS IS A PLAN SETUP FOR A PERSPECTIVE DRAWING

SP

As the rays from the station point go out to the columns that are farthest away from the central visual ray, they meet the picture plane at ever more acute angles. They travel farther to reach the picture plane and are therefore farther apart. The net effect is that the columns in the final drawing get to be thicker and thicker—a fact we know to be not true.

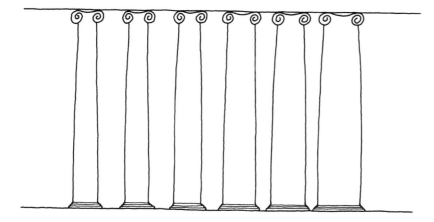

In this way, cone of vision determines how near the station point can comfortably be to the subject of the perspective drawing to avoid distortion. You should note that some distortion—or exaggerated perspective effect—may be useful in certain settings to emphasize relationships of parts or of scale. In general, however, distortion is undesirable in drawing, since it overwhelms the subject.

How far the station point should be from the subject is determined by complex factors involved with the purposes of the drawing. If you want to set your design in context, then clearly you need to step back quite a distance. It may be helpful, if this is your aim, to use a site plan for the plan setup, rather than the main floor plan of your design. Site plans usually show some context and therefore can help you establish distance to the station point by allowing you to set up your cone of vision as described in Chapter 8, while including nearby objects.

If, on the other hand, you want to show maximum detail of your subject, then you will want to place the station point as close to the subject as the cone of vision will allow.

Height above the object is also height above the ground. If you think of the ground as being "normally" about 5' below the eye level of a standing viewer, then traveling up or down from that ground will give you bird's-eye or worm's-eye views of your subject. In the same way that you established the ground plane of the perspective frames in Chapters 7 and 8 by measuring *down* 5' to find where your subject meets the ground, so if you measure 40' (or 100' or whatever suits) down to find that ground, you will have a bird's-eye view. If you measure only 1" down (or less), you will have a worm's-eye (ankle height) view of your subject. Such views can be very useful when your site is on a hill or if you are designing a tall tower to be viewed in the context of a city of tall towers.

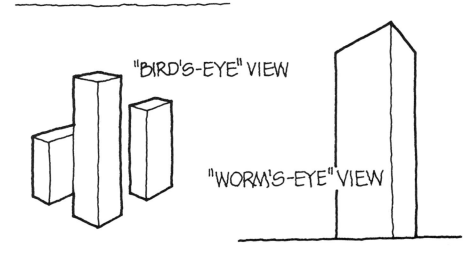

The final difficulty is where to place the station point in relation to the points of the compass. This is totally a factor of the orientation of the building or object you are drawing. Obviously, the center of interest in your design should be in the perspective drawing. This requirement will help you determine the general orientation of the station point. It is a poor idea, however, to place the center of interest directly at the center of your drawing—this will tend to make it seem static and ponderous.

As a frequently broken general rule, it is a good idea to make one set of receding lines in a perspective drawing recede much more steeply to a vanishing point within that drawing than the other, which will, for most rectilinear objects, be far off to either the left or the right. Such placement, again as a frequently broken rule, tends toward dynamic drawings, full of energy and apparent movement. I always suggest to my students at this point that they look at the perspective drawings of any great renderers and artists they admire. The study of *how* they did it is very useful.

INCREASING OR DECREASING THE SIZE OF THE PERSPECTIVE

The perspective constructions we have described so far all depend on the plan-to-station-point-to-picture-plane relationship to determine the final size of the drawings. Though they sometimes produce drawings of an appropriate and useful size, at other times the perspective will need to be adjusted larger or smaller.

Clearly, one way to do this is to move the picture plane while keeping everything else stationary. The internal relationships and proportions in the drawing will be the same no matter where the picture plane is—don't forget the window analogy for the picture plane. Moving it is like moving the window back and forth between you and the object, or into the space occupied by the object, or beyond it. Since the station point is fixed, the rays from it to every important point in the object (review steps in Chapters 7 and 8) will travel farther and be farther apart from each other if the picture plane is moved away from the station point. This makes a larger drawing.

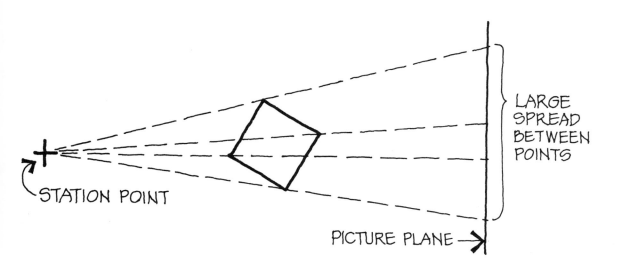

Conversely, if the picture plane is moved nearer, the perspective becomes smaller.

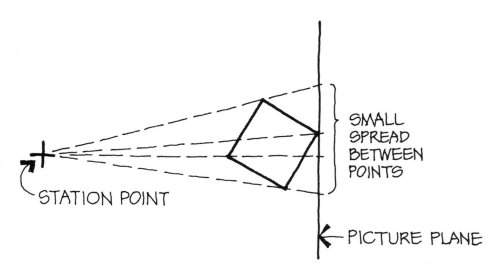

The problem with this movement is that, according to what we have studied so far, the picture plane must be in contact with some part of the object to allow measurement of heights. The solution to the problem posed by moving the picture plane away from contact with the plan is to create "phantom" walls in one-point drawings and "phantom" lines in two-point that serve as walls and lines of true height. They are called "phantom" because they appear in your perspective constructions floating in space between the horizon and your subjects.

CREATING "PHANTOM" WALLS

A phantom wall, the true size of the back wall in the plan setup, can be established by "sliding" the whole room or object back to a distant picture plane in the same way that furniture is "slid" to locate it in a one-point perspective. The process is the same as that described in the first demonstration in this chapter.

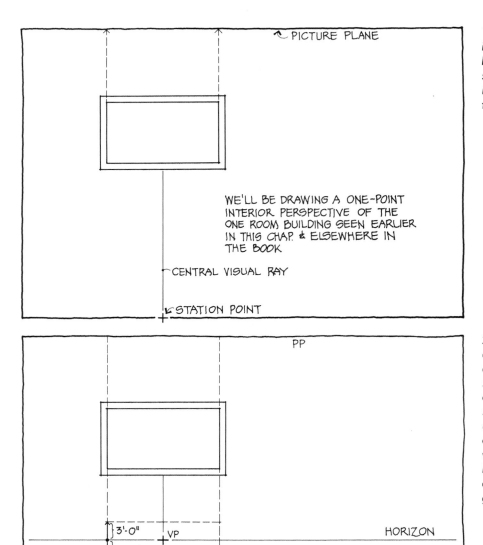

1. Working in the plan setup described in Chapter 7, "slide" the corners of the back wall of your room or object straight back (up the board) until they intersect the picture plane. Use your t-square and triangle for this.

2. Drop these intersections straight down into the area of the perspective drawing. Measure down from the horizon line (established as described in step 6 of Chapter 7) to the floor in the same scale as used in the plan setup. Measure up from this floor line to the appropriate ceiling height. You should end up with what looks like a simple elevation of the back wall of the room you are drawing at the scale of the plan you are using to generate the perspective.

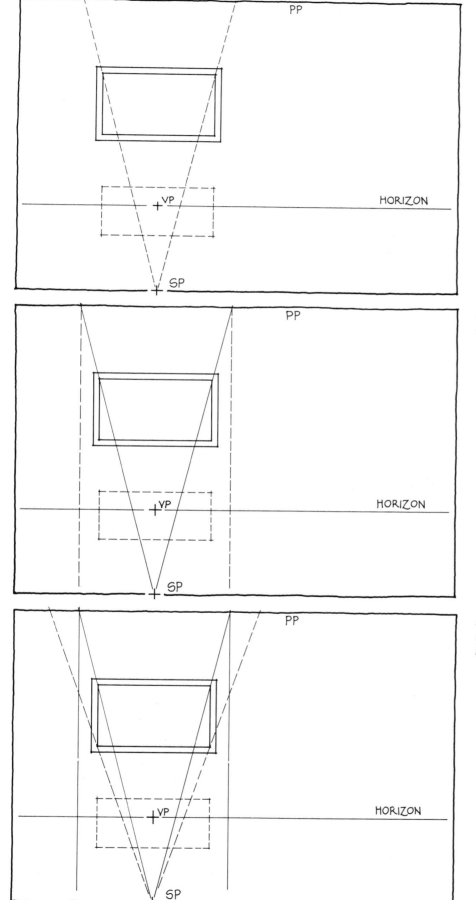

3. Return to the plan setup and project the corners of the back wall of the room to the picture plane. Do this using a push pin at the station point and inverting your t-square to draw lines connecting the station point, the corners of the wall, and the picture plane.

4. Drop these intersections straight down into the area of the perspective.

5. Now project the front corners of the room in the same way as you did the back in 3.

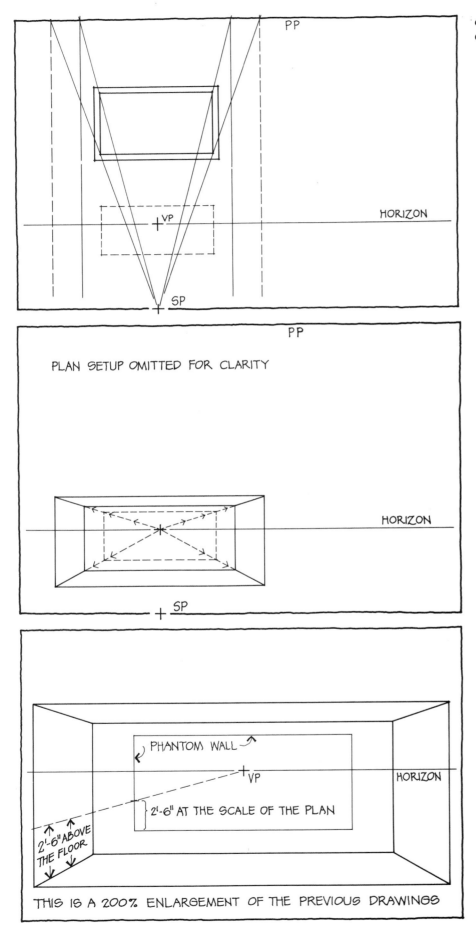

6. Drop these intersections straight down into the area of the perspective.

7. Move the push pin and place it in the vanishing point in the perspective. Using your inverted t-square, connect the vanishing point to the corners of the phantom wall created in 1 and 2. Extend those radiating corner lines until they cross the lines you brought down in 4 and in 6.

8. You should be left with the "frame" of a room in one-point perspective, which has "behind" it a floating wall. When you want to project a height into this perspective room, you need only measure that height at the most convenient corner of the phantom wall, and using your push pin and t-square, project it along a side wall of the perspective frame, and carry it across into the field of the perspective as described in step 6 (on page 110) of the sequence that describes the projection of furniture into one-point perspective drawings earlier in this chapter.

PLAN SETUP OMITTED FOR CLARITY

PHANTOM WALL

2'-6" AT THE SCALE OF THE PLAN

2'-6" ABOVE THE FLOOR

THIS IS A 200% ENLARGEMENT OF THE PREVIOUS DRAWINGS

PROJECTION OF A "PHANTOM" LINE OF HEIGHTS

Though one-point perspective allows you a "phantom" wall, no such luxury is available when you construct in two-point. You will have to settle for a "phantom" line of heights, the background (or foreground) analog of the line of heights described in Chapter 8, step 11. You will have to project and wrap dimensions from it to the points where they are needed in your drawing.

You have already had a taste of the phantom height line in the section on projecting furniture into a two-point drawing, although the idea was not presented per se. We will review and identify it here. We will assume that you have decided to move the picture plane back (away from the station point) in the plan setup to produce a larger final drawing, though it could just as well move forward to make the drawing smaller.

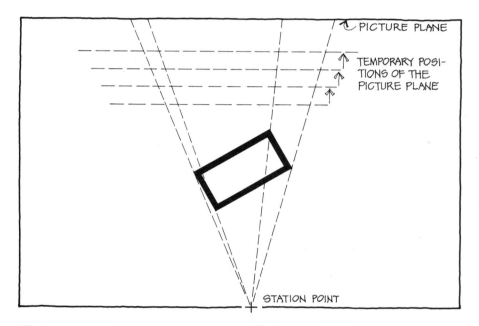

1. Working in the plan setup, establish your station-point-to-object relationship, and project the main corners of your subject, as described in Chapter 7, to a picture plane that you imagine but don't draw. Think of it as sliding back and forth, away from or toward the station point. When the intersections of the projected corners and this imaginary picture plane are about as far apart as you want them to be in the final drawing (that is, at the width you want for the perspective), draw in a picture plane at that location.

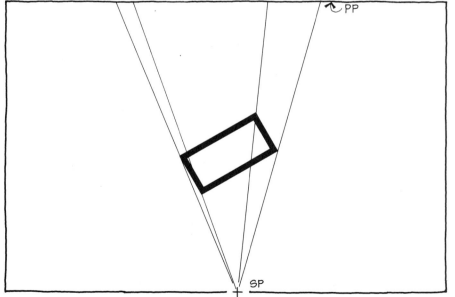

2. Now insert a push pin at the station point, and using your inverted t-square, draw in projector lines connecting the station point to the corners of the subject to the picture plane. This is the same procedure described in step 9 in Chapter 8. I use colored pencils or a 4H lead to make the marks on the picture plane.

127

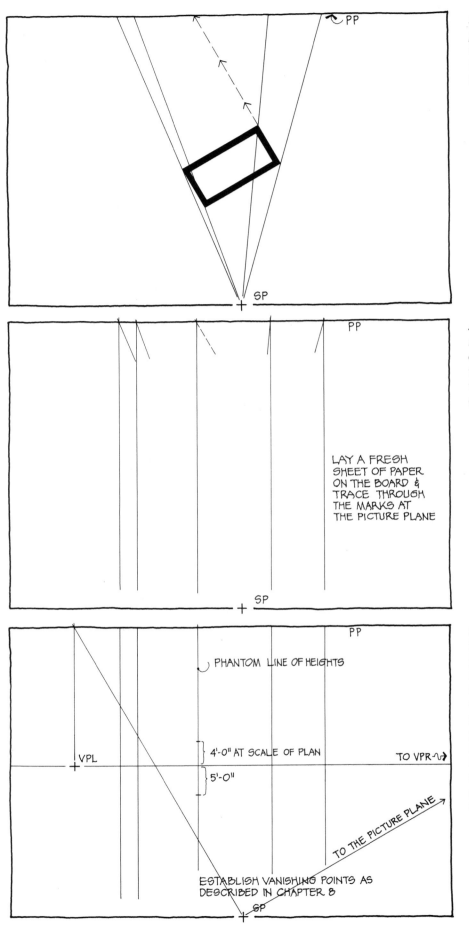

3. While you are still working on the plan setup, draw a line from one side of the subject along the axis of that side. Extend the line until it touches the picture plane.

4. Drop these five points (the four corners and the point found in 3) straight down into the perspective (using t-square and triangle), and continue them down well into the area of the ground in your perspective frame.

LAY A FRESH SHEET OF PAPER ON THE BOARD & TRACE THROUGH THE MARKS AT THE PICTURE PLANE

5. Where the trace of the point you found by extending one side of the subject until it touched the picture plane drops into the area of your perspective, it becomes a line of heights. You may want to think of this line as a corner of your object that has been ''slid'' to the picture plane to establish the same contact it would have if the picture plane had been drawn against that corner in the plan setup. Measure down to the ground and up to the top of your object on this line.

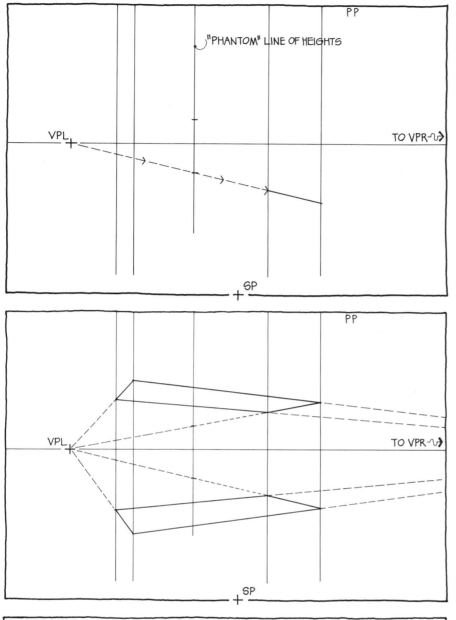

6. Now project these heights onto one of the corners you brought down in 4. Do this by first putting a push pin into either VPR or VPL and using your inverted t-square to connect it to the ground point you just found in 6. Extend the line from that ground point to intersect the trace of the corner of the object dropped down in 4. You choose the vanishing point to use for this according to which direction the side you will draw points.

7. Move the push pin to the opposite vanishing point from the one you just used, and draw the adjacent side of your object. Continue moving back and forth between the vanishing points until you finish drawing the base of the object. Repeat these steps for the top of the object.

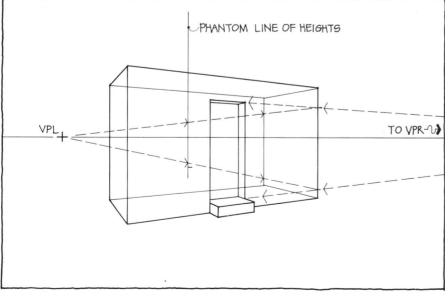

8. Heights within the object must all be scaled along the phantom line of heights and be projected into the area of the object, as was the height of the object itself in step 7. If the phantom line is aligned with a back plane of the object, you will have to wrap the heights around the object so that they will appear on the front. This suggests that, where possible, you should align your phantom line with a front plane.

CHAPTER TEN

LETTERING

The purpose of lettering, like that of drawing, is to communicate. Lettering is used to convey those ideas we are unable to draw or which are more economically and clearly communicated by words. Lettering is therefore vital to a designer—without it our drawings are incomplete.

The imperative to communicate requires that our letters must come close to achieving universal recognition. Though you may have seen many styles used by architects, designers, and drafters, the optimum type of letter over the years has proved to be a simplified Roman (or Trajan) alphabet. These letters have been employed for centuries, they are relatively easy to form, and they are recognized instantly by most Western readers. They have a lot going for them. You should certainly consider learning them before you undertake to imitate some other model—in the long run they all look affected and unnatural. Look at the illustration below for the first models I imitated:

And learn from the advice given me by my first boss, who told me when he saw these awkward letters that I should practice the Trajan alphabet—that once you learn how to make good standard letters your *own* style emerges spontaneously and will be more satisfying than any you might copy. He was right.

LETTERFORM

The key to learning to letter well lies first in learning to look at each letter as a *designed* element and to divorce it from its meaning. This is hard. We start to concentrate on letters and their meanings very early in life and now I am asking you to go against your history. What you must do, however, is learn to think of each letter as a *drawing*. An *A* is a composition in three strokes, each having a definite beginning and ending, the crossbar located at a precise spot between top and bottom. A *B* is a composition including a straight line and two circle-segments of slightly different radii and carefully related proportions. So you won't get anxious, let me assure you that you already know the heights and proportions—looking at the alphabet for as long as you have has forced this information into you. Now you simply need to evoke it.

The second thing you need if you are to letter well is the willingness to practice. Not only the letters are designed, the words they form are too. The space around each letter influences the appearance and readibility of the word, so it too must be designed. Practice in forming letters and practice in assembling those letters into real words, which you design, is the only sure way to master lettering.

Now let's get started. The alphabet below is my best effort to produce a clean, easy-to-read and repeat, simplified Roman set of letters. Note that I learned these letters from other architects and that they have achieved wide acceptance in the profession. This is a Roman alphabet in that the basic letterform derives from the letters found on Trajan's column in Rome, with the serifs (the little crossbars at the ends of most letterstrokes) deleted for the sake of speed. Note especially the proportions of the letters (instruction in their actual formation follows). Each square of the grid surrounding the letters is ⅛″ × ⅛″. The width of the letters varies and is noted below each one. The heights are all about the same, though in fine calligraphy this is not so.

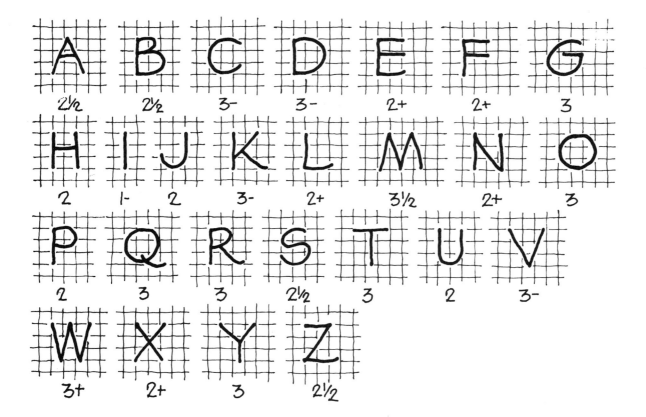

Now that you have learned to see each letter as a drawing, a composition of line strokes, and have studied the proportions of at least one alphabet, you must learn how to form the letters yourself. Start with a comfortable size—say, ½″ or ⅜″ high like the examples. Be sure to give yourself guidelines, which are simply parallel, horizontal lines between which you form the letters. They will help you achieve letters that are uniform and professional-looking. Follow the sequence of strokes shown below. The arrows show the direction of the pencil or pen stroke; the numbers before each stroke give the sequence.

Note that different methods exist—what I am showing below is how I make the letters. Left-handed people may want to experiment with the sequence so they don't carry their hands across the strokes already laid down; there are some notes just for them later in this chapter. You may find it more comfortable to make your *O*s in two segments (like the circular portion of my *Q*s). In the end the differences are less important than finding the sequence that works for you and then practicing.

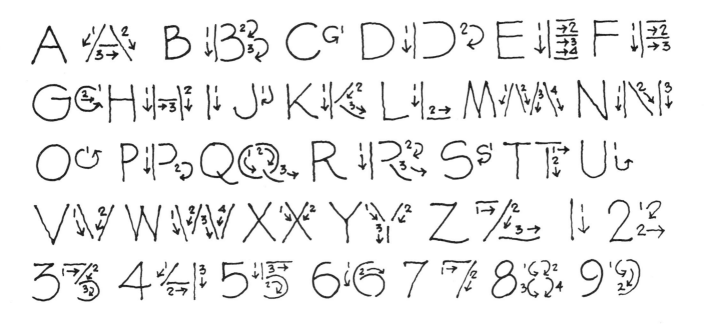

LETTERSPACING

After you learn to see and form the letters, the hardest aspect of learning to letter is understanding the spaces required between them when they are combined into words. This is very much an area of art; what we must deal with is proportion, judgment, prejudice, and style. The letters and spaces that satisfied my father's generation look stilted and mannered to my eyes. How will mine look to my children? Nonetheless, it is useful to learn the biases of your times, if only to improve your ability to communicate.

It is alluring in this regular world to think that all letters should be spaced equally far apart. That notion dies early, however, when looking at a word with *L*s or *J*s or *I*s in it. If you measure the space to the next letter from the farthest extension of these letters, the space between them will look vast when you finish. The word falls apart, with awkward visual gaps in the middle. Communication is hampered, not aided.

A second notion of spacing is based on the premise that each letter should be placed within an envelope of space that is the same as that surrounding every other letter. This does not, of course, yield equal spacing between letters, since they have different widths. Though equal spacing was not what we sought, the random spaces that do occur between letters arranged by this system are most unpleasant and again yield words that fall apart or are crowded together.

What we must find, then, is a pleasing rhythm of contained space—the area inside the letter—to amorphous, partially bounded space—the area between letters.

One school of thought recommends that the total visual area between letters be the same. The visual area includes some of the space that open letters—like *C*s and *F*s—contain but don't enclose. To my eye this organization produces unsatisfactory anomalies, especially around the letters *I, L, J, Y, T, A,* and *V.* The space around these letters either seems too large, in the case of the *I* or *T* or *L* or *J,* or it slips away, in the case of the others.

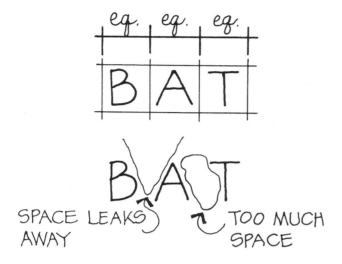

What is needed is proportional spacing in which the letters accommodate one another. However, no very good rules exist here. The problem, of course, is that most situations are unique, and generalized recommendations are therefore hard to make. To my eye, for example, the letter *I* requires less space around it than most of the other, "squarer," letters. Combinations, like *AV,* require less space between letters than, say, an *RM* combination, because the former pair have complementary slopes and need to snuggle. The best way to learn what works for your eye and lettering style is to practice words, not just alphabets. As I sit in meetings or talk on the telephone, to this day I still practice my lettering. It is the only way I know to make it good and pleasing to the eye.

BAT WINDOW ELEVATION

WINDOW ELEVATION FACADE

FIRST FLOOR PLAN SITE PLAN

SECTION PERSPECTIVE

SOME RULES ABOUT LETTERING

A good deal of wisdom has been collected about lettering on drawings. I will simply list some of it here, in no particular order.

1. Use a relatively soft lead. The softer leads are less likely to get caught by the paper grain and will allow you a smoother stroke.

2. Letter last. You are less likely to smear that way. On a complicated drawing you will need to know where the lettering can go, and this is only apparent if you letter last.

3. Use guidelines. They are indispensable if you are to make regular letters. We all use guidelines all our working lives.

4. Make each "bar," or element, of your letters with a single, bold stroke; broken elements look weak and disheveled.

5. If you draw a malformed letter, it is generally better to leave it and go on than to try a repair. It will become lost in the verbiage.

6. Begin practicing with letters in the 3/8"-to-1/2"-high range. Make smaller letters as you gain confidence with the larger ones.

7. Avoid slanting your letters. It is almost impossible to make the slant uniform.

8. Don't rush.

9. Cover what you have completed with pieces of yellow trace. They will help keep your drawing clean.

LEFT-HANDED LETTERING

The greatest difficulty in lettering for those who are left-handed is in keeping the completed letters from becoming smudged. There is no easy solution to this problem. What I do recommend, however, is that you note especially 9 above: cover what you have done so the heel of your hand won't rub over it. Some of my friends rest their hands on small triangles as they work. The triangle keeps their hand above the paper, while not presenting a visual barrier.

   A further point, and perhaps a more important one, is that you should *not* attempt to imitate the motions of your right-handed friends. Experiment to discover what motions work best for you. I have discovered from observation that lefties draw the crossbars of their letters from right to left, whereas righties draw them from left to right. This suggests that it may be better for you to draw the crossbars first and join them later with the vertical elements, unlike the sequence shown above. The illustration below suggests an approach.

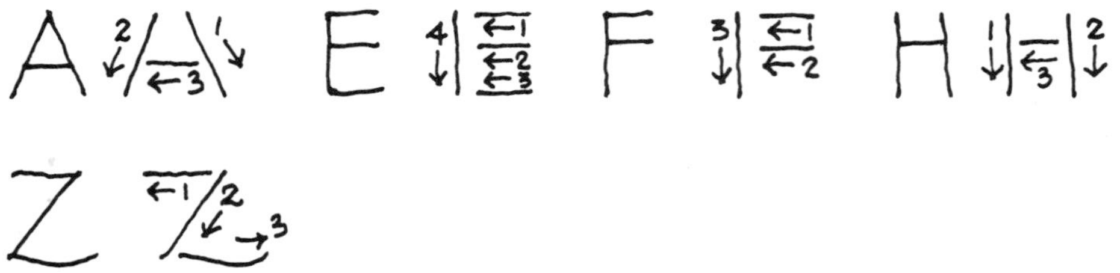

CHAPTER ELEVEN

MODELMAKING

In a sense, models are the most eloquent presentation form available to designers. No matter how good their drawings, they are illusions. (By that I mean the illusion of three dimensions attempted in two.) Models are simulations and as such often convey a better idea of a design than drawings alone can. Of course, designers may have time to make only one model—or none—and their presentations will therefore always include drawings, which are still the quickest and cheapest way to provide multiple views of an intended space or object. They are also the most accurate way to describe a design. A well-scaled, adequately detailed model, however, is without peer for presenting a design.

There are really only two categories of models that are generally recognized: study models and presentation models. General agreement ends here, and it is sometimes hard to know where a study model starts becoming a presentation model. Usually, study models are cruder in their fabrication, may lack all surface detail, and frequently aim at exploring only one quality of a design—often the massing.

Presentation models, on the other hand, are usually larger, are made of more different materials, and may reproduce considerable detail in a rather complex effort to present the look and "feel" of a building or space. A still more elaborate form of modeling is the full-size mockup of a piece of a building (or of an entire object, in the case of industrial designers) in the effort to study some particular fact or facts.

We can only begin to explore model making here, so we will concentrate on the ones that are most useful to students. This will also put a limit on the materials and tools we will look at; few students have the time, tools, and skills to work on machined, "hard" models.

SOME VERY IMPORTANT CAUTIONS

It is important to recognize the dangers of modelmaking: extensive use of cutting tools is required. Students tend to work late at night, when their reflexes are slowed by fatigue. This is the worst possible time to construct a model—the cardboards are heavy, the knife drags, a slip can sever a tendon. Remember: *Don't work late or when you are tired.*

A further caution: dull knives (and other blades) are a greater danger than sharp ones, because they present wider surfaces (being blunt) to the material grain or texture and hence can deflect more easily. Note: *Use sharp blades and change them often.* Don't "make do" here—the cost of the doctor and of the healing time will far outweigh any minor economies you may make. Keep a whetstone (even the free ones sports shops give away with a new pair of ice skates will do) on hand so that if you run out of new blades, you can sharpen the dulled edges frequently.

On heavy materials *do not attempt to cut through with one pass* of your knife—make several light passes. When you bear down hard to cut through with one pass, your muscles cramp and stiffen, and you lose some control of the knife. This will ultimately mean that the knife will wander from the line you want it to follow. At the least this will ruin some material and slow the job. A light touch will enable you to control the knife almost as you do a pencil. The job will, in the end, go faster if you follow the seemingly slowest route.

TOOLS

To make models you will need some tools that you may not already own, so I will describe them here. They include cutting tools, straightedges to cut against, glues, and clamps.

No. 1 Modeling Knife Handle. X-acto and other makers supply a small handle that holds blades of several different shapes. It is universally referred to as a "no. 1 handle." Generally, only one blade shape is useful, the no. 11. I buy them in quantities of ten. They are used to make detail cuts and small openings, since they are acutely pointed, and are well-suited to making inside corners, as at window openings.

Mat Knife. A bigger handle that holds regular mat-cutting blades is made by many manufacturers. The ones I like best are by Stanley or by Lamb (illustrated). The blades they hold are of standard shape and are widely available. They are used for long cuts in heavy materials.

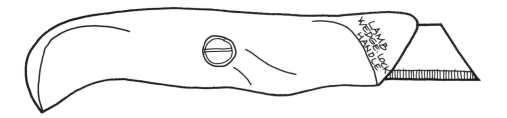

Zona Saw. For cutting small pieces of wood you will need a model-maker's saw, usually called a "Zona" saw. Several manufacturers offer this type of saw; look for one with a stiffened back and a very thin blade with exceptionally fine teeth (approximately 40 to the inch).

Hot-Wire Cutting Tool. If you will be making study models of building masses, you may well decide to make them of Styrofoam (polystyrene foam) blocks, cut quickly with a hot wire. These tools can be homemade or bought ready-made. The former are much cheaper than the latter, though they require some small skill in electrical assembly. Avoid the fumes of the heated Styrofoam—they are apparently very toxic!

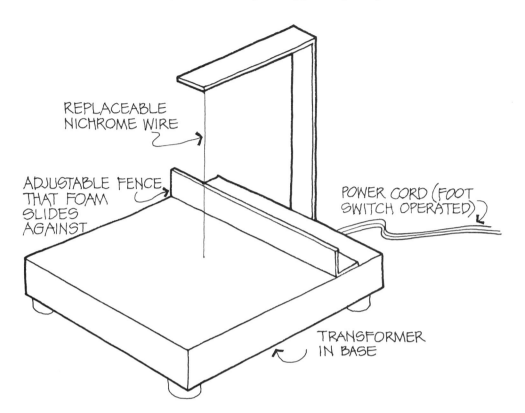

REPLACEABLE NICHROME WIRE

ADJUSTABLE FENCE THAT FOAM SLIDES AGAINST

POWER CORD (FOOT SWITCH OPERATED)

TRANSFORMER IN BASE

Aluminum T-Square. You will need a metal t-square. The aluminum kind is cheaper than the stainless steel kind. They both look just like a t-square, only made of metal. They are used for making long cuts and for laying out the model.

Stainless Steel Ruler. You will find a metal ruler very useful for shorter cuts. Mine is a stainless steel model 18″ long, made by Pickett. It has a cork composition backing that keeps it from slipping around. This is a most important feature.

Aluminum Triangle. To cut small pieces, you will need an aluminum triangle. Since it is lightweight, you can use a relatively large one to cut small pieces. Mine is 12″ on its long side.

Cutting Board. For years I used scrap pieces of cardboard to protect my drawing surface when I made models. The cardboard needed to be replaced fairly frequently since otherwise it became scarred and pulled the knife away from the line I wanted to cut. In recent years cutting boards of high-density polyethylene have been available, and I have taken to using one. They are easy to store and self-healing (somewhat), so that previous cuts don't draw your blade (the problem all cutting surfaces have at some time or other). They are expensive, so you may need to resort to the "scrap" cardboard cover.

Mitre Box. A modelmakers' mitre box can be very useful, though it is not absolutely essential. Joints depend largely on the area joined for their strength. If two surfaces can be mitred, they present a greater area to each other and hence sustain a stronger bond. With small pieces that will be stressed in any way, it is always a good idea to mitre the joining surfaces.

Glues. Most of our work can be held together with white (polyvinyl acetate) glue. This is available from many makers, including Borden and Uhu. It is water soluble when wet, and transparent and fairly waterproof when dry. Since its medium is water, it will make lighter materials stretch. Be careful when working with large pieces of paper or cardboard and white glue, since once wet with the glue the weight and softening effect of the water can cause the paper or boards to stretch. The more permanent companion of white glue is aliphatic resin glue, which is yellow, dries cloudy, and is stronger and more durable than the whites.

Rubber cement is also frequently used in modelmaking, although it is a very unsatisfactory product in the long run. Its major deficiencies are that it is highly flammable and that its bond is fugitive, lasting only a few weeks. However, it is workable, which means that you can stick something down with rubber cement and work it into position. (This is only true if you put the cement on one of the two pieces to be joined and bring them together while the glue is still wet.)

Cyanoacrylate glues ("magic" glues) are very useful. They will glue most nonporous materials but don't work on many plastics, and they are—magic. Observe all manufacturers' cautions—it is painful to unglue yourself from your model. Lately, cyanoacrylate glues have been available for porous materials (though I haven't had a chance to try them yet).

Spray adhesives are offered by several manufacturers and are very handy for mounting drawings or prints on cardboard or for cardboard to cardboard—in fact, for laminating any relatively smooth, porous sheet materials. Their bond is not durable in my experience, however, and the adhesives in some cases "blush" through paper materials. They are also expensive. I think of the spray adhesives as a lazy person's rubber cement.

Clamps. A clamp can be anything that holds materials together while their glues set. For us that can mean pins, rubber bands, drafting tapes, clothes pins, books, or actual metal clamps. It is a good idea for you to have all the above. The metal clamps I recommend have a jaw opening of about 1½″. X-Acto makes some plastic clamps I haven't used that look as though they could do the job.

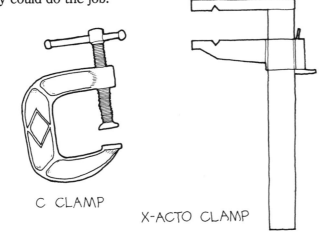

C CLAMP

X-ACTO CLAMP

Vise. A small vise is frequently useful in assembling parts that are later applied to the larger model. Several types are available, including one with a vacuum base, which only works on a smooth surface such as Formica. (I can't imagine what you would be doing working on Formica as you make a model, since the knives we employ are sharp enough to scar and ruin even melamine plastics.) My vise has a screw clamp on its base that allows me to attach it to a work top as thick as 2½".

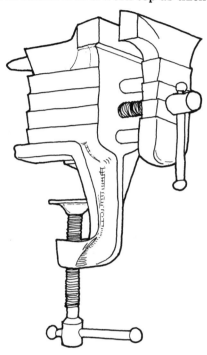

Tack Hammer. A small hammer is useful for driving pins into dense layers of chipboard or for attaching the model to a wooden base. A tack hammer such as upholsterers use is ideal for this and has the added benefit of a magnetized head to hold those little steel nails and pins your fingers are too big to manage.

Pliers. A pair of pliers is almost indispensable. I regularly use two kinds: a lever-locking plier (now available with a long nose from Petersen Vise-Grip) and a conventional needle-nose plier. Of course, there are other tools you may need at one time or another. Most of them are conventional (in the sense that they can be found in a home tool box), and you may well own them already.

MATERIALS

The variety of materials useful in the construction of models is endless. What I will describe here is the core group that seems to have won general acceptance over the years. Be on the lookout for ordinary materials to use in novel ways that may make your production job easier.

Clay. Plasticine is used by some people to make initial massing study models. It is the least architectural of materials, though, in its inherent softness and plasticity. Its main virtue is that it is relatively quick to use. Many people are allergic to it, however, so be aware of this potential drawback.

Styrofoam Blocks. Because of the problems inherent in clay mentioned above, many people prefer to make their study massing models out of white Styrofoam (polystyrene foam) blocks. These create a cream cheese universe, but at least they are hard-surfaced (relative to the clay) and sharp-cornered. You can use scrap packaging material for this purpose (if you can find it in big enough pieces), but the blocks purchased from artists' suppliers are denser and more uniform. They are best cut with a hot-wire tool, described above.

Chipboard. Chipboard is a dense, gray cardboard, prized for study models because of its uniform, anonymous nature as a material. It doesn't look like anything except chipboard. A more polished (and somewhat denser) version is known as "bookbinders' board." The only place I've ever found to buy it is a bookbindery.

Chipboard comes in a variety of thicknesses, which ultimately means that you can find an appropriate thickness of board so that even small-scale study models (usually made out of a single layer of board) can nonetheless have a realistic wall thickness.

The problem with these materials is that their density and grain or texture resist the knife, so considerable effort is involved in cutting them. Though we will talk again about cutting in general, the key to using these boards is to cut through them with multiple passes of the knife, as described previously, and *not* to attempt to cut them with a single pass and great effort.

Foamcore. Foamcore is the now-generic name of two products of interest to modelmakers. Both are boards made of a sandwich of two paper faces laminated to a polystyrene foam inner layer of various thicknesses. One of the boards is a kraft-paper-faced foam board, the other a plate-bristol-board-faced foam board. The kraft-faced board is brown like butcher's paper, with a white core. The plate-bristol-faced board has a smooth, hard, white face and a white core. They are both paramount materials to amateur modelmakers (all of us who don't make our livings at it) in that they are easy to work, are well-suited to modelmaking, and are usefully sized. We'll go into more about them later.

Illustration Board. A white cardboard of great usefulness, available from several makers though usually referred to as "Strathmore board," is a fine presentation model medium. Be sure to specify "illustration board—Strathmore drawing board," made up of several layers of rag-based drawing paper. It is very expensive and also well-suited to modelmaking. The illustration board is made of two layers of Strathmore paper bonded to a white cardboard substrate of several thicknesses. It provides a cream cheese alternative to the chipboard models we will discuss. Since its surface is the same as that of Strathmore drawing paper, it is possible to intermix the two and achieve a great range of thicknesses. This fact has led to a whole new style of model in the last ten or fifteen years or so that is as abstract as the designs it represents. The models have more in common with the paper the architecture is drawn on than with the reality of building they both show.

Plastic and Wood Structural Shapes. Several makers supply shaped sticks that are useful in the construction of architectural and design models. Those shapes are usually made for railroad or other hobby models and are frequently found at hobby shops. Some artists' supply shops sell them, and some have a large enough clientele to have shapes made for architects alone. In any case, no matter where you live, look in a drafting supply catalog, a hobby store, or the ads in model railroad or airplane magazines for shapes that can represent beams, columns, and other linear elements.

The Human Figure and Other Scale-Giving Factors. Just as human figures are essential in sections and other drawings to give scale, so are they useful in models. The simplest way to show them is to use figures cast to scale in lead or gun metal that are now generally available. They can be bought at most artists' and architects' suppliers and provide a reasonable expression of scale. An alternative (and the only way to show the figure in large-scale models) is to find appropriately sized figures in magazine illustrations, laminate them to cardboard, and prop them up in your models.

Model cars, trucks, buses, boats, airplanes, park benches, street lights, furniture, and so forth can all be purchased in cast metal. They can be used as is, with their dull metallic sheen reinforcing their abstraction, or they can be painted with nonglossy modelmaker's paints.

Trees also help provide scale and context and are an eternal problem to modelmakers. Lichen is packaged and sold for use in model railroads, and it makes a good shurb for architectural models, but a terrible tree. Its scale and texture are not right for trees and look too chunky and dense. The best, and most believable, material for trees is something I know only as "graveyard weed." Ask around for it; some drafting supply stores carry it.

DECISION-MAKING CHECKLIST

More than anything else, the production of a model takes planning. By planning I mean thinking through all the steps from choosing the type of model to make, to buying your supplies (for instance, most artists' supply stores are closed on Sundays), to the actual manufacture of the model. Decide on the materials that are appropriate for your situation. Evaluate the amount of time available to you. Think about production—how will you *make* it? That includes the step-by-step procedures for manufacturing the pieces themselves. Decide in advance how you will account for the thickness of the materials. What sorts of joints will you use? What kind of glue? Make an inventory of materials on hand. Will they really be enough?

After this period of planning, I return to the beginning and ask myself whether the initial decision as to model type is still realistic. How long will it really take to make this model? Do I have that much time, and if I do, is that how I want to spend it? Once I have answered these questions and settled on the type of model I both want to and can make, I go through an actual written inventory to make sure I have every essential. A series of questions follows that will assist you in making an exhaustive checklist.

1. Do I have the necessary amount of board stock, whether chipboard, illustration board (and/or illustration paper), or foamcore?

2. Do I have the basswood or plastic beams and other premade parts my mental image calls for (such as cast figures)?

3. Do I have the appropriate glue or glues, and are they fresh and useful? (Glues dry, even in closed containers, and lose their workability over time.)

4. Do I have the tools I will need? (These include the ones described above and any special ones you may know you will need.)

5. Do I have an adequate cutting and assembly surface?

6. Do I have an adequate nearby reference surface on which to rest my drawings as I build the model?

7. Do I have a plan of action for the manufacture and assembly of the model that presently exists only in my mind?

THE PLAN OF ACTION

The planning of a model is a separate and distinct procedure from the planning of a building. Like cabinetmakers, modelmakers need to prepare lists of materials that show each piece to size, taking into account the materials' thicknesses. Fortunately for us, the lists of materials can be laid out directly on the board stock we will eventually cut up to make the model.

What I do is lay a sheet of the board stock I am using on my drawing table and square it up to the t-square. Then, having calculated from my design drawing the approximate linear length of "wall" I will need, I convert that dimension to actual (full-size) inches. If that length is within the width of my board, I simply draw a single line parallel to an edge of the board and the height (to scale) of my model's walls. The height you use is a factor of how you have visualized and are constructing the model. In general, it is a poor idea to have the floors come through to the outer wall of a model, so the walls should run the full height of the building or object you are modeling. In this case, the walls need to be laid out first, and the floors and roof fitted to them.

You may find that the edges of the board have been damaged in transit from the factory to your workplace. If so, you will want to draw a line to guide you in cutting off the damaged selvage. Use that line as the point of origin for laying out later lines. If I will need more than one stock wall strip, I draw another line below the first. Be sure to lay out plenty of wall strips; there is always a certain amount of waste when you come to the end of the strip.

Now lay out the floor or floors on your board. You must remember to subtract the wall thickness all around from the overall dimensions of your building. Since the materials we use almost never are precisely the right thickness, it is a good idea to lay out your model pieces working from outside dimensions in. To conserve material, try to nestle the shapes together. Lay out any other pieces you will need.

HEIGHT OF WALL ⬍   ⌐SCRAP

HEIGHT OF WALL

HEIGHT OF WALL

FLOOR 1 | FLOOR 2 | FLOOR 3 | SCRAP

WINDOW & DOOR LINER STRIPS

CUTTING

At the risk of being repetitious, let me again urge caution and respect for the cutting implements. I have known several people who have hurt themselves badly while modelmaking, and the damage can be permanent.

In cutting sheet materials, always run your knife along a metal straightedge. On occasions I have fooled myself into thinking I was exempt from this rule. Every time I have done so I have ruined a perfectly useful plastic straightedge. The metal edge should be thick—at least ⅛"—if you will be making long cuts. The straightedge functions in two ways: to guide the cut and to protect your fingers. The thicker edges are harder for the knife blade to leap over—a safety factor—and they are more likely to keep your knife vertical—an important consideration when you later measure to that cut or glue something to the edge. Whenever possible, place the metal straightedge on the part of the material you will use, and let the scrap, or the part not yet allocated, stick out on the far side. In this way, if your knife wanders, it will ruin material you haven't yet invested time in.

Stand in such a position that your stroke can be made smoothly, with nothing hindering its completion. Now, using the mat knife for long cuts (over about 18") and the no. 1 knife handle and a no. 11 blade for shorter cuts, make the cut. Draw the knife toward you, along the opposite side of the straightedge from the one your holding arm is on. Start the cut at the farthest point from you on that line, preferably at an edge. If you are working in chipboard or other resistant material, make several light passes along the straightedge, one after the other without moving it. On lighter (less resistant) boards and on shorter cuts, you may find a thin-gauge aluminum triangle an adequate guide. In these cases, where the long muscles of the arm can control the cut fairly easily, the reassurance of a thick straightedge isn't necessary.

JOINTS

The biggest problem when planning and making models is joints. They must be designed for adequate strength, which is a factor of surface area in the joint. The greater the area the greater the strength. Joints must be allowed for when laying out the panels before cutting.

There are three fundamental conditions that concern us: right-angled joints, edge-to-edge joints, and point-to-plane joints. The joints most frequently used (because they solve the problems we encounter with the least effort) are called: butt, lap, and rabbeted.

Butt Joints. Butt joints occur where edges abut edges in the same plane. They are least commonly used in modelmaking because the panels we use are so thin that their edges do not provide enough surface area to glue adequately, and the joint they make is therefore not strong enough. It may happen, however, that you need to join two panels together either because the stock you are using is not big enough for the project at hand or because you are running out of material. In either situation, I recommend that you use a scrap strip running the full length of the joint to back it up and that you glue it along its entire surface (however, this is technically no longer a butt joint).

Where a column or beam meets a plane is also strictly a butt joint, and such points of contact are also hard to make strong. You can do so when you are working with a thick material or with a built-up wall model (described below) by allowing the column or beam to penetrate the top skin of the foamcore or built-up material and by gluing it to the foam or both layers of the chipboard.

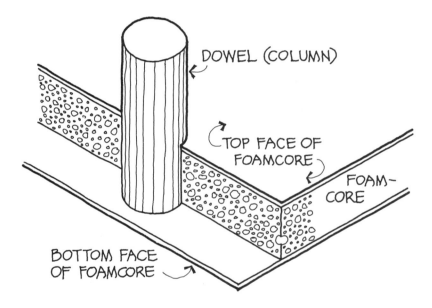

Lap Joints. Lap joints are used in the construction of chipboard and foamcore study models. They are simple, right-angled edge-to-edge joints that depend for their integrity on the strength of the glue. (Lap joints, in the sense of two panels being overlapped, are almost never encountered in modelmaking.) Since there is relatively little surface-to-surface contact in these joints, it is best to back them too. The simplest way to do that is to use a ⅛″ × ⅛″ (or ¼″ × ¼″ if the model's size allows) balsa wood stick along the length of the joint. The wood should be glued securely to both panels it abuts.

The only other lap joints commonly used occur in relatively large-scale models made of such material as foamcore, the thickness of which will allow you to make a simple joint that will have enough internal area to survive for a while. But it probably won't withstand a trip from your home to school if it gets jostled around. The next type of joint solves this problem and is also useful in making presentation models.

Rabbeted Joints. A rabbet (spelled "rebate" in British English, but pronounced "rabbet" in both languages) is a right-angled cut along a corner edge of a panel by which enough material is removed so that the corner can accommodate the fitting in of the adjacent panel's edge.

Rabbetted joints are the strongest generally used in making board-stock models. They typically present about twice the surface area for a joint than a simple lap-jointed corner would and therefore make very strong joints.

In a model that has walls built up of several layers of board stock (or built up as a hollow panel as described below), rabbeted joints are extremely useful. Their construction in chipboard will be described in the section on built-up models.

Model Types Useful to the Student

As mentioned earlier, there is no general agreement on nomenclature in the field of modelmaking. Realistically, there are really only three types of models that students are likely to make. They are solid mass models, like clay or balsa block models; skin or sheet models that utilize one layer of cardboard or thin plastic stock; and built-up wall models that also use card or plastic stock. Solid mass models are useful as study models; they are almost never appropriate for presentations. Single-skin models are useful as both study and presentation models, and built-up wall models are almost always of presentation quality if only because of the time invested in them.

Massing Models. Massing models are useful for studying the bulk, volume, or shape of a building or object in its context. They are always study models. As a general rule they do not include the building's openings (doors and windows). These models show mass in the dictionary sense of expanse or bulk. The appropriate materials to use in making a massing model are clay, Styrofoam blocks, and wood blocks (only balsa wood is easy to work and therefore truly appropriate for a do-it-yourself model).

Single-Skin Models. Other study models are used by designers to study form and proportion. They are made of (relatively) easily cut and manipulated sheet materials such as gray chipboard or foamcore. A single layer is used, since only the envelope and mass need be suggested, not wall openings and surface thickness. Workmanship is often crude; the panels of the model are frequently cut and recut as the design is developed and refined. The lap joint is most appropriate for this type of model.

Single-skin construction can also be used to make presentation models. This is especially true where the model is of small scale, and the sheet stock used for its construction approximates (to scale) the design thickness of the walls. In these models the fabrication should be more careful than in study models, and openings and some surface detail will usually be shown.

Foamcore is eminently well suited to the fabrication of single-skin presentation models since it is of substantial thickness and can be readily worked to create the strong, rabbeted joints described above. They are relatively easy to make. You make a cut on the inside face of a wall panel that is parallel to the edge to be joined and one material thickness in from that edge. You must be careful to only cut through the top layer of bristol board or paper and the foam's middle layer. Do not cut or score the outer layer of board or paper. You now need to run your no. 11 blade down the joint pointing into the foam layer and immediately adjacent to the outer layer of board or foam. This second cut will detach the foam and inner piece of paper or board you no longer need. You are left with a rabbeted edge, ready to receive the adjacent panel. The whole process is easier to do than to describe and is illustrated here:

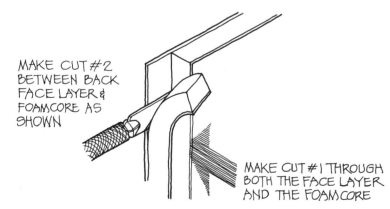

MAKE CUT #2 BETWEEN BACK FACE LAYER & FOAMCORE AS SHOWN

MAKE CUT #1 THROUGH BOTH THE FACE LAYER AND THE FOAMCORE

The other great attribute of foamcore is that its surface can be drawn on to suggest surface detail that is otherwise too shallow to show in the model. The bristol-board-surfaced material is ideal for this, although the brown butcher paper surface will also withstand being drawn on. I find that the best medium for such drawing is ink, which because of its bold contrast with the board surface is well adapted to abstract detail.

Built-up Wall Models. Where the scale of your model is too large for single thickness materials to satisfactorily simulate a wall, you will need to build up panels. This is somewhat more time consuming than the simpler methods previously described, which is why this form of modelmaking is appropriate to presentation models. In brief, what is involved is the creation of hollow wall assemblies constructed of inner and outer layers of sheet stock held apart by edge and spacer strips. The inner and outer layers need to be of different lengths so as to create the rabbeted corner connections previously described.

The procedure involves a plan of attack, as always. First, decide which set of walls will be fit inside the other. They should be made up as a simple pair of panels, with both the outer wall surface and the inner of the same length. That length equals the *outside* dimension of your building minus the thickness of two layers of the stock you are using.

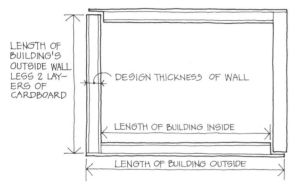

The manufacture of the other two walls is somewhat more elaborate, since they include the corner joints. In this pair of walls the inner panels are the length of the building's outside dimension *less* the thickness of the walls. The outer panels are the length of the building's outside dimension. The fit of the four walls just described looks like this:

147

The only really difficult part of manufacturing this type of model is keeping track of where you need to subtract the stock thickness and where you don't. It is easy to forget, when you are dimensioning panels, that you must subtract the designed wall thickness *twice* from the inner panels—once for the left-hand wall and once for the right.

BE SURE TO DELETE THE THICKNESS OF THE OVERLAPPING PIECES WHEN YOU LAY OUT THIS WALL ↲

Once you have figured out the dimensions of the various panels, cut the stock to height out of the full width of your material. This gives you long pieces to cut the walls from and ensures that the various panels will be the same height. If you need two or more "wall" lengths, cut them to height with great care so that they will be of uniform dimension. Next, cut a lot of strips that are the thickness of your model's walls, minus the thickness of two layers of your stock. These are the pieces that you will use to close up the wall's edges and to separate the two wall panels. They will also serve to line all openings for windows, doors, and so on.

It is a good idea to brace the liners and edges as you assemble your panels. I like to do so with the corners of scrap pieces of the stock I am using. I simply hack off corners on the diagonal, ending up with a triangular gusset piece I dip in the glue and shove into position beside the strip I need to brace. These pieces add significantly to the strength of the total assembly and should not be neglected.

Weight the panels with books while the glue dries. A layer of ordinary waxed paper between the books and the panels will ensure that the glue doesn't seep out and ruin both.

When you have completed the panels of your model, you must assemble them so that the corners are square. This is relatively simple if you are gluing the walls to an accurately cut floor, but that is not always the sequence of events. When I am assembling walls with rabbeted corner joints but no reference angle to assure their trueness, I use a small, old acrylic triangle no longer useful for drawing to check the inside angle. A clean carpenter's square will do the job as well.

Making Curves

Sooner or later you'll design something that requires a curved wall or portion, and you will confront the problem faced by all curve-makers in a rectilinear world. Our materials are flat!

To make a curved plane out of a lightweight cardboard you need to make many small score marks on its backside. The marks can be made with a knife, in which you run the risk of cutting through the board, or they can be made with a fine ballpoint pen, which must be born down on. Think of making a model of a drum. If the cardboard represents the sides of the drum, then the score lines should run up and down those sides.

Once the cardboard is scored you should gently roll it over the edge of the table so the board can fold a little at the score marks. Hold the card so the score marks are parallel to the edge you are rolling the board over and are on the underside of the board. Now glue the curved plane to several cardboard disks you have prepared that are two-cardboard thicknesses smaller in diameter than the finished drum. The disks help the curved plane maintain its shape and keep it from bellying.

If you are working with thicker boards you will need to take chunks out of their backs instead of simply scoring them. In foamcore boards I do this by laying out locations for surgery with my drafting tools and then making two cuts at 45° to the surface and removing a triangular strip.

Curved planes made with foamcore need to be supported just as those of cardboard do.

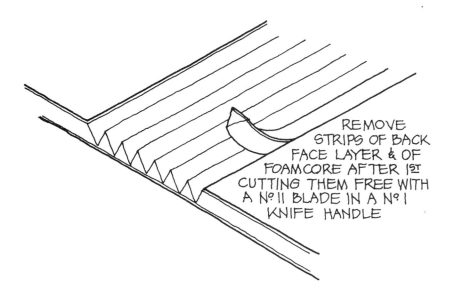

REMOVE
STRIPS OF BACK
FACE LAYER & OF
FOAMCORE AFTER 1ST
CUTTING THEM FREE WITH
A N° 11 BLADE IN A N° 1
KNIFE HANDLE

GLOSSARY

All terms defined herein are italicized in the other entries.

Axonometric drawings are also frequently referred to as "paraline" drawings. The root words of "axonometric" mean "measurable along the axes." Axonometrics are oblique views of a building or object that give a "fake" perspective in that they don't obey all the laws of optics.

Every axonometric drawing includes three axes that correspond to width, depth, and height. Each line drawn parallel to these axes is scalable, meaning that it can be measured with a scale throughout its length. (Not all axonometric drawings use the same scale on each axis, however.) Angles between the axes of axonometric drawings correspond with those of our drafting triangles, making the construction of an axonometric drawing fairly simple.

"Axonometric" refers to a whole group of *drawings,* including *isometrics, dimetrics,* trimetrics, and so forth. A second meaning of the label "axonometric" is also applied within this group to oblique views of objects or buildings that include angles of 90° between any two adjacent walls. Such drawings usually are constructed over *plans* that have first been rotated through an arc of 45° around one corner.

Central visual ray lies at the center of our visual field. It is so-called because of the rays of vision that people in the middle ages thought were sent by a viewer to an object. In a *perspective drawing* this line is placed by the drafter to connect the center of interest with the *station point.*

Charrette was the wagon used in the École des Beaux-Arts to collect student work when due. It was named for the wagon used to carry prisoners to the guillotine for execution. To be *en charrette* therefore meant to be working feverishly to a deadline, literally, "in the wagon," presumably on the way to execution. It still does. Those French students were cards.

Cone of vision is that segment of the field of view within which an object in perspective will look "right"

to a viewer, and beyond which it will appear to be "distorted." The label "cone of vision" is a useful reminder that the eye is a ball and sees both up and down and side to side. It sets our drawing limits and corresponds roughly to our field of view when the eye and head are held still.

Convergence is the tendency that parallel lines moving away from the viewer have to appear to get closer to one another until they seem to merge—and ultimately vanish. It is an essential attribute of *perspective drawings.* (See also *Diminution, Foreshortening,* and *Superimposition.*)

Dimetric drawings are oblique views and a type of *axonometric drawing.* They are prepared with two different scales so that, for example, distances along the front plane are shown true to scale and those along the receding planes are shown at two-thirds that scale to produce a false diminution. *Diminution* is one of the principal characteristics of *perspective drawings* and is missing from axonometrics unless it is induced in some artificial way (such as by using two different scales). A drawing of this type is called dimetric for "two measures."

Diminution is possibly the most necessary attribute of *perspective.* It refers to the fact that objects appear to become smaller as they are farther away from us. The brain interprets this into other kinds of knowledge—how far away something is and what its relationship is to other objects in the field of view. (See also *Convergence, Foreshortening,* and *Superimposition.*)

Drafting is the creation of drawings with tools, that is, t-squares and triangles. Such drawings have very straight lines and very smooth, even circles and curves.

Drawing is the act of representing an object with lines and sometimes tones that are manually created. This therefore includes both *drafting* and *sketching.*

Elevations depict the facades of buildings or objects as though the designer were suspended directly in front of each building element and at right angles to the principal plane of the drawing. Think of Peter Pan or of hummingbirds here, able to dart about to each part of the subject and examine it head on.

Entourage refers to everything surrounding a drawing's subject. It comes from the French for "around," in the sense of "in the vicinity." This includes all the objects, forms, and surfaces that place a drawn building or object in context in the world and that give it scale. Such material can often make an otherwise ordinary drawing wonderful. It is essential where an object's size is otherwise not apparent.

Foreshortening is the compression and change in apparent geometry that occurs when an object is rotated in our field of vision. It is one of the essential attributes of *perspective drawing* (see also *Convergence, Diminution,* and *Superimposition*). Think of a pencil or a book turned to an oblique angle in relation to your face. The pencil loses length, the book height.

Horizon line is needed in every perspective, whether it appears in the final drawing or not. It is simply the eye level of the drafter. The horizon line is important in making *perspective drawings* since lines in the foreground that continue into the middle- and background all converge to a point or points on the horizon.

Isometric drawings are oblique views and a type of *axonometric drawing.* They are constructed from design dimensions taken from plans and sections. An isometric drawing includes angles of 120° between its right and left front walls instead of the 90° that axonometrics include (see the second meaning of *Axonometric* above). This type of drawing is as popular as the axonometric.

The word "isometric" means "equal measure" and is derived from the theory underlying this drawing type (that is, axonometric projections).

Models are miniature simulations that help us understand the volumes and masses we design. Drawings, after all, are illusions representing three dimensions in two.

Models are also used to present designs to the nontechnical public who may not fully understand drawings.

Oblique drawings are the second large category of drawings (after *orthographics*) and are made by rays that meet the drawing paper at angles other than 90°—hence the name "obliques." The most familiar of these are *perspectives.*

Axonometric drawings, which supply oblique views of subjects, are in fact orthographic drawings of objects seen obliquely. They are not, therefore, oblique drawings as defined above. (See *Orthographic drawings* and *Perspective drawings.*)

One-point perspective is one type of perspective drawing. Perspectives are categorized according to the number of *vanishing points* used in their construction. The vanishing point is a concept central to the understanding of perspective. In one-point perspective drawings subjects are oriented so that one of their major planes is parallel to the drawing's surface. Lines in that plane are considered to recede to vanishing points that are infinitely far to the right and left and that are therefore ignored. The other parallel lines in the drawing—those at right angles to the *picture plane* that appear to move into the perspective—are all drawn converging to a common vanishing point on the *horizon.*

Orthographic drawings are made by rays (see *visual rays* and also *projections*) that meet the paper only at right angles. (The word "orthography" has roots in Greek that mean "right drawing.") These drawings provide flat, true-to-scale images of the object drawn. Such views are seldom seen in nature, except of very small objects.

Plan, section, and *elevation drawings* are orthographic drawings, as are *axonometrics.* Even though the category includes axonometrics, people generally understand you to mean plan, section, and elevation when you refer to orthographic drawings or projections.

Perspective drawings are another category of the *oblique drawings* described above. They closely approximate much of our seeing and therefore are most understandable to most viewers. Perspectives conjure up in the viewer's mind an impression of the built design. Quite in addition to their value as tools for communication with others is their value as tools for the design process.

Perspectives have three properties that no other design drawings have: *convergence, diminution,* and *foreshortening.* These properties make the perspective realistic where *axonometrics* are stilted and artificial.

Picture plane refers to the concept of a drawing as capturing a scene on an imaginary plane between the observer and the subject. The word "perspective" comes from the Latin "see through." Understanding of perspective began with the notion of a window located between the artist and the subject. The subject was "seen through" that window. The artist could take a crayon and draw the scene on the glass. It was a short leap from this understanding to the substitution of paper for the glass. The paper, being opaque, had to be held out of the artist's line of vision. The glass was labeled the "picture plane," since it was in the plane of this window that the drawing was supposed to be made. Its exact corollary was that piece of paper under the artist's drawing hand. They are interchangeable except for the fact that the paper was opaque.

Plans are frequently referred to as "floor plans," though they in fact represent horizontal cuts through buildings at windowsill height (about 3 feet above the floor). All material above the cut (with a few minor exceptions) is considered to be discarded, and the designer (and the viewer) is therefore able to look directly down into what remains—that is, the floor surrounded by 2- to 3-foot high stub walls.

Poché comes from the French *pocher,* to blacken an eye, and is used in English as "to poché," meaning to blacken in, as the thickness of a wall to make it read as solid. Another piece of French gallows humor.

Presentation drawings are design drawings for presentation to clients or teachers. They may be: *sketches,* if they help explain the development of your thinking; *drafted drawings,* if the design is sufficiently refined to be best explained by them; or freehand *tracings* over previously drafted drawings.

Projections are so called because they are based on the theory of projection that underlies technical drawing. Orthographic projection theory holds that each point on the object drawn is "projected" to the *picture plane* by a ray that meets the picture plane at right angles and that is parallel to the projector rays of every other point.

Rendering is the embellishment of a drawing with lines and tones for any of several reasons: "holding" surfaces, creating surface texture and detail, illustrating materials, simulating the play of light. The word is also used as a noun to refer to a rendered drawing, as in the statement, "I'll take that rendering to our client meeting."

Sections (also called "vertical sections") are the vertical equivalent of the horizontal slice that makes a *plan.* Here too whatever is on the viewer's side of the cut is discarded, and we are able to look directly into the building. This is a lot like looking into a doll's house—everything is revealed in miniature.

The section is inextricably linked to the plan and to the designing of volumes. It is developed at the same time as the plan. Coupled with a plan or plans, it helps the viewer understand the volumes of a design. It gives a great deal of information about the qualities of a space and the heights of sills and other mundane pieces of building shown on the plans.

Sketching is drawing by hand and pencil, without using other tools and without wholly copying or *tracing* another drawing. Note that a sketch may be partly traced, but it must somewhere involve new thought. Even if it is partly traced it represents a developing idea, which grew out of what was drawn before.

Station point is the viewpoint, that is, the point from which the view is made. Think of making a photograph; at the instant you press the shutter release, you take a picture from where you were standing. In *perspective drawing* the equivalent position is traditionally called the "station point"—presumably because the drafter is stationed at that point while constructing the perspective.

String is, in the jargon of architects and builders, a series of dimensions along a line. One example is the dimensions along a wall plane: you measure first from a corner to a window, then across that window, then across the piece of wall between that window and the next one, and so forth until you come to the end of the wall. String dimensions are usually shown on measured drawings laid out along one line; this helps make the drawing tidy and quickly readable.

Superimposition is an important aspect of composition, not an inherent optical quality. It is the overlapping of objects in the visual field. It gives us important depth information, which in turn helps us determine the size of unfamiliar objects.

Three-point perspectives are constructed like two-points except that because the observer is positioned looking up or down at the subject (for some pictorial reason determined by the drafter), a third *vanishing point* is needed for the vertical lines. Since these lines are not parallel to the *picture plane* (as they are in *one-* and *two-point perspectives*), they converge to a third vanishing point.

Trace means to copy through a translucent medium such as tracing paper. A second meaning, which you will find in this book and most others on *perspective* and *oblique drawing* generally, is that of the mark (usually a line) which a *visual ray* makes as it passes over the ground (often the drafter's paper) between its point of origin and its ultimate intersection (such as with the *picture plane* or the *horizon line,* with another line, and so on). The word is French and comes to us from the École des Beaux-Arts. In France *trace* means "trail," "spoor," or "faint track." The nearest equivalent in English is "construction line." Both appear in drawings being developed, neither, as a rule, in *presentation drawings*.

Two-point perspective is a type of perspective drawing. Perspectives are classified according to the number of *vanishing points* required to make them.

Two-point perspectives are the most familiar of all drawings. By definition both major horizontal axes of the subject in a two-point perspective must lie at oblique angles to the *picture plane*. This means that each appears to converge to a different vanishing point on the *horizon*. Hence the name.

Vanishing point(s) differentiate *perspective drawings* from all the other drawings we have studied. Every set of parallel lines in a perspective drawing except those parallel to the *picture plane* converges to a vanishing point. They are usually on the *horizon line*.

Visual ray is a line connecting the observer and any significant point on the object observed. The rays also intersect an imaginary plane called the *"picture plane"* needed in the constuction of a *perspective drawing*.

SELECTED BIBLIOGRAPHY

CHAPTER ONE
THE BASIC TOOLS AND MATERIALS

Charrette Corp. **Annual Catalog.** Woburn, MA. *A standard for the industry. The business was founded by architects for architects. This company is one of the few to realize that students will one day be professionals—they take good care of all their customers. At this writing they have retail stores in Boston (three in the area), New York City (two), and New Haven.*

Teledyne Post. **Drafting and Repro Products Catalog.** Chicago, IL. *A widely available catalog of general drafting and other supplies. Teledyne relabels many makers products, so this catalog is of broader interest than those of most manufacturers. The equipment shown is also widely available, another distinct advantage.*

CHAPTER THREE
THE BASIC DRAWINGS

Ching, Frank. **Architectural Graphics.** New York: Van Nostrand Reinhold Co. *A basic book on design drawing.*

Forseth, Kevin. **Graphics for Architecture.** New York: Van Nostrand Reinhold Co. *Though Forseth addresses the beginning student, his book is also useful to someone who wants to study drawing theory. Can serve as a reference to drawing types.*

Martin, C. Leslie. **Design Graphics.** New York: Macmillan Publishing Co. *An excellent, somewhat dated textbook on design drawing. Useful as a reference to drawing types. Excellent section on shadow casting.*

Ramsey & Sleeper, et al. **Architectural Graphic Standards.** New York: John Wiley & Sons. *The profession's standards, assembled in one place. Without peer as a compendium. Terribly expensive.*

CHAPTER FOUR
LINES, TONE, AND RENDERING

Atkin, William Wilson. **Architectural Presentation Techniques.** New York: Van Nostrand Reinhold Co. *A useful book that reproduces many wonderful drawings and is relatively affordable. The chapters on pencil and pen rendering (2 and 3) are helpful. The pages on the structure of trees (86 and 87) are worth memorizing.*

Doyle, Michael E. **Color Drawing.** New York: Van Nostrand Reinhold Co. *A first rate book on drawings made with spirit markers and colored pencils.*

Halse, Albert O. **Architectural Rendering.** New York: McGraw-Hill Book Co. *This was the standard in the field for years. It is now somewhat dated and needs more demonstrations of how to do what is illustrated.*

Oles, Paul Stephenson. **Architectural Illustration.** New York: Van Nostrand Reinhold Co. *A book by one of the most successful renderers around. Makes a convincing argument for the value of perspectives in the study of light in and on buildings.*

Porter, Tom, and Bob Greenstreet. **Manual of Graphic Techniques.** New York: Charles Scribner's Sons. *An excellent modern book that describes a huge range of graphic techniques in appealing visual form. For the person who already knows something about drawing.*

Porter, Tom, and Sue Goodman. **Manual of Graphic Techniques.** New York: Charles Scribner's Sons. *Same comments apply as for the above book.*

CHAPTER FIVE
AXONOMETRIC DRAWINGS

Forseth, Kevin. **Graphics for Architecture.** *Described above under Chapter Three.*

Martin, C. Leslie. **Design Graphics.** *Described above under Chapter Three.*

CHAPTER SIX
GENERAL INTRODUCTION TO PERSPECTIVE

D'Amelio, Joseph. **Perspective Drawing Handbook.** New York: Tudor Publishing Co. *This curious little book, though somewhat dated, is a good beginner's handbook. Now out of print, but well worth looking for in second-hand stores.*

Doblin, Jay. **Perspective.** New York: Whitney Library of Design. *Another way to construct a perspective drawing. Something of a classic.*

Gill, Robert W. **Basic Perspective.** London: Thames & Hudson. *The rather austere drawings and unfortunate book design hurt the clarity and simplicity of Gill's approach. An excellent primer that needs its companion volume (listed under Chapter Nine below) since no method for embellishing a drawing is described in this book.*

Lockard, William Kirby. **Drawing As a Means to Architecture.** Tucson, AZ: Pepper Publishing. *This book is a classic of brevity, clarity, and intelligence. Lockard makes the case for a freehand perspective technique that results in accurate renditions of the design. He further advocates the use of one drawing and writing implement, an inexpensive cartridge fountain pen.*

Rich, Steven. **Rendering Standards.** New York: Van Nostrand Reinhold Co. *Does for rendering what* **Graphic Standards** *does for architectural information generally.*

CHAPTER SEVEN
CONSTRUCTING THE ONE-POINT PERSPECTIVE

D'Amelio, Joseph. **Perspective Drawing Handbook.** *Described above under Chapter Six.*

Gill, Robert W. **Basic Perspective.** *Described above under Chapter Six.*

CHAPTER EIGHT
CONSTRUCTING THE TWO-POINT PERSPECTIVE

Burden, Ernest. **Architectural Delineation: A Photographic Approach to Presentation.** New York: McGraw-Hill Book Co. *An alternate approach to constructed perspective that involves photographing a study model in lieu of all the steps of perspective construction. This method can have real advantages if you have the photographic equipment you will need and are making a model anyway. You can pick the best station point visually.*

D'Amelio, Joseph. **Perspective Drawing Handbook.** *Described above under Chapter Six. Explains three-point construction.*

de Vries, Jan Vredman. **Perspective.** New York: Dover Publications, Inc. *Some wonderful Renaissance drawings.*

Gill, Robert W. **Basic Perspective.** *Described above under Chapter Six. An excellent explanation of three-point construction.*

CHAPTER NINE
DETAILS WITHIN THE PERSPECTIVE AND EMBELLISHMENTS TO IT

Gill, Robert W. **Creative Perspective.** London: Thames & Hudson. *Gill gets around to telling you how to furnish your perspectives.*

CHAPTER TEN
LETTERING

Durer, Albrecht. **Of the Just Shaping of Letters.** New York: Dover Publications, Inc. *(from the* **Applied Geometry of Albrecht Durer,** *vol. 3). A serious study of the Roman (or Trajan) alphabet, with construction methods for each letter. Regretably, Durer's compass did not make round circles, so it's a little hard to copy him. Durer's alphabet is unsurpassed.*

Goudy, Frederic W. **The Alphabet and Elements of Lettering.** New York: Dover Publications, Inc. *Two books published as one by a 20th-century master of type design. The plates at the end are worth the price of the book and are reproduced by Dover as their Foot-High Letters series.*

CHAPTER ELEVEN
MODELMAKING

Hohauser, Sanford. **Architectural and Interior Models: Design & Construction.** New York: Van Nostrand Reinhold Co. *The only useful book in this neglected field.*

INDEX

Edited by Stephen A. Kliment and Susan Davis
Designed by Jay Anning
Graphic production by Katherine Rosenbloom
Set in 11 point Century Old Style